It's a Wonderful Life

Serving God Joyfully in Marriage and Ministry

Terrie Chappell

First published in 2006 by Striving Together Publications, a ministry of Lancaster Baptist Church, Lancaster, CA 93535. Striving Together Publications is committed to providing tried, trusted, and proven books that will further equip local churches to carry out the Great Commission. Your comments and suggestions are valued.

Striving Together Publications
4020 E. Lancaster Blvd.
Lancaster, CA 93535
800.201.7748

Edited by Danielle Chappell and Cary Schmidt
Cover design by Jeremy Lofgren
Layout by Craig Parker
Proofread byEsther Brown, Winifred Brunston, Danny Coats, Agnes Huffmaster, Julie Jenkins, Kristy Kelly, Amanda Michael, Sarah Michael, Suza Rasmussen, and Brenda Yarborough

ISBN 1-59894-008-2

Printed in the United States of America

DEDICATION

To Paul—my husband, best friend,
and counselor. I admire you and love
spending my life with you.

ACKNOWLEDGEMENTS

This book is the result of the efforts of many people.
I sincerely thank each one.

All the glory belongs to the Lord. Without Him, life would
have no purpose or meaning. I thank the Lord for answering
prayer and giving direction during this project.

To my husband—my greatest supporter and advisor.

To Danielle, Larry, Kristine, and Matthew for being the best
kids a mom could ask for and for your patience, sacrifice, and
support during this project. (Danielle, thank you for all your
help in editing the book.)

To Cary Schmidt—thanks for encouraging me
every time I wanted to quit and for your helpful
insight and recommendations.

To Shirley Bianco, my mom, for your prayer support.

To our many volunteer proofreaders who spent
many hours making this book better!

To all the ladies of Lancaster Baptist Church—I love
serving the Lord with each of you.

A special thanks to the ladies who attend our Ladies' Bible
Study and to the wives of our deacons. Thank you for your
constant prayers and words of encouragement, especially
throughout this project.

And finally, thanks to you—the reader. I pray this book
will encourage you to experience the wonderful life
God has designed for you.

Table of Contents

FOREWORD

*I*t has been said that behind every great man of God stands a great woman. Never has this been more true than in the marriage and ministry of Dr. and Mrs. Paul Chappell. If you have never had the privilege of meeting or getting to know Terrie Chappell, then you must know a few things about her before you delve into the pages of this book. Simply put, her godly spirit, her unwavering support of her husband, her sacrificial heart towards the ministry, and her unselfish love for her family, her church, and her husband cannot be overstated. Terrie Chappell has been, for twenty-five years, a model pastor's wife. She is a true portrait of Christian grace and godliness, and she personifies the character of Christ and a heart of compassion and commitment in every area of her family and ministry life.

Terrie Chappell came by faith with her husband to Lancaster, California, in 1986. At that time, the Chappells invested all of their savings into moving and establishing themselves in a rented apartment in a delapidated section of downtown Lancaster. Twelve people had voted unanimously for them to come to the Lancaster Baptist Church. The church offered no salary and could not even pay their moving expenses. Once they arrived, they discovered that the church building was in foreclosure and for sale. The church had a terrible testimony with community leaders and businesses alike.

The devil fought the Chappells in many ways and tried to discourage them during their first few days of ministry in Lancaster. During their first week, while Pastor Chappell was out soulwinning, a lady approached the apartment door and asked to speak to the pastor's wife. When Mrs. Chappell came to the door, the lady stepped inside and had a drug-induced epileptic seizure in the entryway of her apartment. This was Mrs. Chappell's "welcome" to Lancaster!

In those first few weeks, vandals broke into the church, gunshots rang out in the neighborhood, and kitchen cabinets often became discouragingly bare. Through all of this, God protected and provided for the Chappells, and Mrs. Chappell continued to support her husband and love the Lord. During the first months of ministry, the church telephone rang at the Chappell house, and Mrs. Chappell served as a full-time wife, mother, and church secretary. She did the bulletins, the stat sheets, and taught Sunday school children from nursery through sixth grade.

In time, the church was able to hire additional staff, and Mrs. Chappell took a more focused role in the ladies' ministries of the church. In 1992, she began a ladies' class for single mothers and ladies whose husbands did not attend church. She began aggressively winning ladies to Christ—teaching and discipling them personally in their Christian faith. Within just a few months, this class was averaging sixty ladies in attendance, and God was doing a marvelous work through Mrs. Chappell's godly life.

Since that time, Mrs. Chappell has led the ladies' ministry of the church without ever receiving one paycheck. She now oversees multiple ladies' classes at multiple Sunday school hours; she daily coordinates ladies' activities, retreats, and a weekly Bible study; and she handles various counseling matters.

In addition to this, Mrs. Chappell opens up her home and her heart to the entire Lancaster Baptist Church and West Coast Baptist College family. In any given month, she serves as hostess to hundreds of people. She and Pastor Chappell have literally been given to hospitality as nearly every Sunday evening families, students, and Christian leaders gather in their home for a time of food, fellowship, testimonies, and spiritual nurturing. This kind of servant's heart and transparency is foreign in many ministry circles today, but it has consistently characterized the ministry of the Chappells at Lancaster Baptist Church. Our church family is blessed to have this kind of leadership in a pastor's wife.

For the past twenty years, the Lancaster Baptist Church family has had the privilege of calling Mrs. Chappell our pastor's wife. She has given herself in Christ-like service and surrender in more ways than can be described in these brief pages. She has supported her husband on the mountaintops and in the valleys. She has loved her family and kept their needs at the forefront of her heart. She has constantly opened her heart, her home, and her entire life to new Christians and to the rapidly growing church family at Lancaster Baptist Church.

During fellowships at her home, she can be found in the kitchen serving, preparing, and giving of herself to other ladies. When it comes to ladies' ministry, she can be found counseling, planning, teaching, studying, and in hundreds of other positions of service and self-sacrifice. She has given herself to a tireless, unceasing effort of labor and love from her heart. She is a sweet-spirited woman with Christ-like character, and she epitomizes the meek and quiet spirit that the Apostle Paul exhorted godly women to possess.

Quite honestly, Terrie Chappell would have been the last person to assign this book project to herself. Her meek spirit would not have allowed her to presume this kind of influence; yet, those of us who know her are convinced that the world needs more pastors' wives like her.

In the pages of this book, you will see the heart of a lady simply following God and trusting Him on a journey that is quite unpredictable. You will discover the heart of a woman following her husband's faith, doing her best to fill that ever-growing position of influence that God has put before her. You will enjoy the illustrations and personal stories. You will enjoy the insight and the "inside look" at Mrs. Chappell's heart for ministry. Most of all, the biblical principles will stir your life and challenge you to truly be a selfless servant of Jesus Christ.

Every church deserves a pastor's wife like Terrie Chappell. The message of this book is the message of her heart and life. It is our prayer that this book will compel you to go and serve your Lord, your husband, your children, your church family, and the ministry that Jesus Christ has called you to with the same fervor and spirit that Terrie has exhibited. May God grant you a fresh vision, and may He ignite your desire to live more fervently and more passionately in the cause of Jesus Christ.

It is with great joy that we heartily recommend the pages of this book and the heart behind it as a worthy example. Thank you, Mrs. Chappell, for giving the Lancaster Baptist Church family your sweet spirit and your surrendered life for the past twenty years. Your influence on our lives, both personally and through your husband's ministry, defies description. Thank you for taking time to write this book to encourage others in the work of the Lord Jesus Christ.

Sincerely,

The Lancaster Baptist Church Staff, Deacons, and Church Family

INTRODUCTION

*I*n the early twentieth century, two Russian brothers decided to migrate to America. With the political dangers at the time, they could not go together. So the older brother, Sergei, left Siberia for America first and was required to leave his brother behind. Before leaving Siberia, the two brothers worked out a code that would enable them to communicate about life in America, knowing that they would not be able to write letters to each other.

Once he arrived and settled in America, Sergei would simply send a photograph of himself back to his brother. If life in America was not as good as they both had heard, he would have his right hand in his pocket. If life in America was as good or better than they had heard, he would raise his right hand in the photograph.

After many months of anticipation, Sergei's brother finally received the photo. To his surprise, Sergei was standing on a table with both his hands raised in the air!

If someone were to take a picture of me depicting my life as a pastor's wife using the same "code," I too would be on a table, both hands raised in the air! (No, I'm not charismatic!)

I want to begin by letting you know that I love the Lord. I love my husband. I love my kids. I love the ministry God has given to us. I love being married to the best pastor in the world, and I love being a pastor's wife.

Does that mean that every day is a "tabletop, hands raised" experience? Absolutely not! Some days, it seems like I'm under the table with my hands covering my head! Yet, through it all, God has never failed me, and He has always exceeded my greatest hopes and dreams in the ministry.

In this book, I will attempt to share with you what happens in the life of *this* pastor's wife. I pray it will be a help and benefit to you, whether you serve the Lord as a single woman of God, as a woman married to a godly layman in the church, as a staff wife, or as the pastor's wife. My prayer is that whatever you do for the Lord, you will do it with all your heart, mind, and soul.

It is not my intention to tell you how to live your life or how to do your ministry. I simply want to share some ideas and Bible principles that have worked for me and perhaps to allow God to encourage your heart through the ministry blessings and burdens of my journey.

Quite often, my husband and I take guests to a local Chinese buffet for a Sunday afternoon meal. It's really a wonderful setup. We pray at the table and make our way to the food line where we each get to choose what we put on our plates. As we all head back to the table, I usually notice that none of our plates look the same. We each took what appealed to us.

Please approach this book as a kind of "ministry buffet." You will find some ideas that look appealing and useful. Please take those ideas and apply them as God gives you the ability. If you see something that won't work for you, then don't put it on your plate! Leave it for someone else. (Oh yeah, don't forget the "buffet's golden rule"—take what you like, but please don't spit on the rest!)

As of this writing, my husband has served as the pastor of Lancaster Baptist Church for twenty years. When we came to Lancaster, we had no idea how God would bless or what His true plans were. We only knew that we were stepping out in faith, and we were trusting God to provide. We had a great desire to reach people and to disciple them in their relationship with the Lord, and we knew that the people of Lancaster desperately needed a Bible-preaching church.

Over these twenty years, the journey has been more than we could have ever imagined—both with the blessings and the burdens. I'm sure Sergei's journey to America was much the same—a day-by-day adventure filled with both unexpected blessings and trials. Yet, God has never failed us. He has sustained, strengthened, and supplied every step of the way.

It is my prayer that as you read these pages, you will be strengthened and encouraged for your journey, and that in your "life picture" you too will be "standing on the table—both hands raised"!

Enjoy!

Therefore seeing we have this ministry, as we have received mercy, we faint not.—2 CORINTHIANS 4:1

CHAPTER ONE

Defining a Godly Wife

*S*everal years ago, when our daughter, Danielle, was two years old and our son, Larry, was just a baby, I was standing in the church lobby chatting with several of the young staff wives as we waited for our husbands after a Wednesday evening service.

One of the ladies asked, "Did you hear they caught the serial killer?" I didn't even know there was a serial killer on the loose! We did not have a TV at the time, nor did we get the newspaper—I was all ears. But every time the lady said "serial," I heard "cereal." Now, I know I am a blonde, but I do know the difference between serial and cereal—most of the time. As a mother of two children under the age of two, I was home all day feeding them Honey Nut Cheerios, and had little contact with the outside world.

Everyone was listening intently as this lady told the story. Yet, while I was listening, questions were developing in my mind that nobody else seemed to be asking. When curiosity finally got the best of me, I blurted out in front of God and everyone else, "Why do they call him a 'cereal' killer?" Unfortunately, I didn't stop there. I continued, "Did he leave a certain brand of cereal at the crime scene, or did he steal his victims' cereal? Were the victims covered in cereal?" None of the ladies bothered to answer me because they were too busy laughing hysterically.

I learned an important lesson that night: make sure everyone is on the same page before opening your mouth.

So before I go any further, I want to make sure you and I are on the same page!

My Testimony

I did not grow up "in the ministry." I was not even born into a Christian home. One Saturday afternoon, when I was a child, a man who called himself a "bus captain" knocked on my door and invited me to ride his bus to Sunday school. His church was having a special day, and anyone who rode the bus would receive an ice cream treat. I loved ice cream, so I was very willing to ride the bus. Sunday morning came, and I did not get up in time to go to church. The following week, the bus captain invited me once again. I still did not ride the bus the next morning. Thankfully, this persistent Christian servant did not give up on me. He came to my house three Saturdays in a row.

I finally rode the bus to Sunday school the following morning. I wish I could say that I went to church for a spiritual reason, but honestly, the treat was my motivation! After Sunday school, I went to the bus and waited for the other children to arrive, not realizing that there was a church service too! An usher found me moments later and took me to the main auditorium. I sat on the back row, and for the first time, I heard that I was a sinner in need of a Saviour. After the message that morning, the preacher gave a salvation invitation, but I was too afraid to walk down the long aisle. I went home that day knowing I needed to accept Christ, but not knowing exactly what I should do next.

Several days later, two ladies from the church came to my home to share the Gospel with me. A few moments after they arrived, I prayed and asked the Lord to save me!

As I grew in the Lord after my salvation, I dreamed of one day marrying a godly man—but not necessarily a pastor! It was years later that God finally impressed upon my heart that I was going to be a pastor's wife. I never felt that God had called me to marry a pastor, but I knew God had brought my husband and me together. God is sovereign, and when He called my husband to pastor, I was a part of the package, and my calling was a part of his calling.

My new role as a pastor's wife was not a surprise to God, though it was terribly intimidating to me! Yet, I knew that with God's calling comes God's enabling, and you can be sure that I had every intention of holding Him to His Word!

Defining a Godly Wife

In those early days of preparing for and serving in ministry, I often wondered, "What is a pastor's wife?" I really didn't know any pastors' wives personally, so I made up my own definition: she must be godly, play the piano, sing like a bird, teach Sunday school, run the nursery, know the answer to every Bible question, never make a mistake, and never have a bad hair day.

Other people had similar opinions also. This is the "ideal pastor's wife"—one size fits most:

> Wanted: We want a pastor's wife who is a good
> musician. She must be able to play the piano and
> organ, direct the choir, and plan all the special music.
> She must also be a superior Bible teacher. She must
> head up Vacation Bible School, be knowledgeable
> about our missions work, and plan the program for
> the ladies' missionary group. Of course, she must be
> a well-qualified counselor, since she will be expected

to spend hours every week counseling church ladies through their problems. We also expect her to spend a large amount of time on visitation.

I think the following definition best describes the "ideal pastor's wife" in terms of a desired goal. I hope, whether or not you are a "pastor's wife," you will share a common desire to be a godly wife in the following ways:

> We want one woman who feels that being the wife of a pastor will give her the opportunity to do the most effective work she could possibly do for the Lord; a woman who is willing to become a student of the Bible; a woman who loves people, finds happiness in visiting with church members, and witnesses to the lost. We seek a woman who wants to teach a Sunday school class, is willing to visit the sick several times each week if necessary (many times it is more suitable for a woman to visit another woman in the hospital than it is for the pastor himself to visit), will not demand a great deal of time from her husband, is a good housekeeper, and desires to be a good wife and mother; a woman who makes herself available to as many of the church people as possible, makes the most of her 'looks' and is always attractively attired, is a good cook and enjoys entertaining, has an outgoing personality, prays for her husband and his ministry, and can know about problems in the church and keep them to herself.[1]

Now, before you get too discouraged, remember this is the "ideal pastor's wife." In light of this definition, none of us have arrived! I do pray, however, that we are all on the same journey to become who God wants us to be for our husbands, families, and churches.

In response to the thoughts and opinions others may have of the Christian wife, let's be realistic. We will never be perfect this side of Heaven, and we will never be able to fulfill every one's expectations. There is not one mold or specific job description that fits all Christian wives. We are all different, married to different men, and involved in different ministries, and living out different purposes. The call of God is unique to each of us!

As a pastor's wife, the most simple definition of my life is as follows:

> A pastor's wife is the wife of a pastor.

Ah, now that's more like it! I think that is my favorite definition!

Have you ever noticed that the pastor's wife is one of the few people on planet Earth who is introduced by her husband's profession? When I am introduced at church as Terrie Chappell, people will often say, "Oh, you're the pastor's wife!"

I looked to see if I could find any books on being a doctor's wife, an engineer's wife, a mechanic's wife, a banker's wife, etc., but I didn't find any such books. The only other "wife" that is closely linked to her husband and to the public is the president's wife. Think about how closely we scrutinize the lives of our first ladies. Our opinions of them (whether right or wrong) always affect the way we think of their husbands. And so it is with you. Since you are a Christian wife, you are a constant reflection of your husband and his life calling, and people are constantly forming their opinions of your husband, your family, and your God by the way they view you. That's just the way life is.

Pleasing Others

As a Christian wife, you will be watched and even judged. Some women consider this to be a negative aspect to being a Christian or to being in ministry, and either they resent it and give up, or, in most cases, they become consumed with trying to please people. Neither response is pleasing to the Lord!

Friend, living your life constantly trying to please others is a good formula for insanity! We've all heard the saying, "You can please some of the people all of the time and all of the people some of the time, but you can't please all of the people all of the time!" How true that statement is! The Bible tells us in Proverbs 29:25, *"The fear of man bringeth a snare."* Please remember that just because others are watching, you don't have to live your entire life pleasing them! Instead, realize that God has given you the privilege of influence. You have the joyful opportunity to influence others for God because you are being watched so closely!

Perhaps you have become discouraged or apathetic because you know you cannot live up to everyone's expectations. Many Christian wives take an "I don't care" or "I'll do what I want" approach to life and ministry, failing to understand the incredible opportunity given to them by God. When you are tempted to become resentful because you think God or others have asked too much of you, remember: "I am in this place because God has put me here. He will adequately enable me to fulfill my role in a way that pleases Him." Let me encourage you—do not sacrifice the privilege of influence on the altar of self-centeredness!

Pleasing God

Our ultimate, driving motivation in life and ministry should be to please Christ—not others. His watchful eyes are the ones that matter! We read earlier that the fear of man brings a snare, but we see in Proverbs 14:26 that *"in the fear of the Lord is strong confidence"*! What an encouragement! We can be confident in our lives and in our service to Christ as we seek to please Him alone.

I like to read Galatians 1:10 every so often: *"For do I now persuade men, or God? or do I seek to please men? for if I yet pleased men, I should not be the servant of Christ."* This verse serves as a checkpoint for my motivations in ministry as I ask myself, "Am I doing this act of service to please men or am I truly striving to be a servant of Christ?" Remember that others may judge you, but you will not give an account to them for how you've lived your life! You will give an account to God.

> *But with me it is a very small thing that I should be judged of you, or of man's judgment: yea, I judge not mine own self. For I know nothing by myself; yet am I not hereby justified: but he that judgeth me is the Lord.*—1 CORINTHIANS 4:3–4

Servant Leadership

My husband often uses the illustration of a triangle to describe leadership. If the base of the triangle represents your rights as an individual, and the sides of the triangle represent your influence on others, the higher you go in influence, the more narrow the triangle—the fewer rights you have as an individual. As you grow in leadership and influence, your responsibility to people becomes more important than your rights. The more your leadership expands, the less you emphasize your rights, and the more you emphasize your responsibility and influence on others.

This is what the Apostle Paul referred to when he admonished us, *"For, brethren, ye have been called unto liberty; only use not liberty for an occasion to the flesh, but by love serve one another"* (Galatians 5:13). He also said in 1 Corinthians 8:9, *"But take heed lest by any means this liberty of yours become a stumblingblock to them that are weak."*

Mature Christian leaders don't say, "I can do what I want." They don't demand rights or abuse liberty; instead, they look for ways to serve others and to draw others closer to God. A spiritual leader is willing to sacrifice a petty "right" in order to further the work of God in the life of another!

First Timothy 4:12 says, *"Let no man despise thy youth; but be thou an example of the believers, in word, in conversation, in charity, in spirit, in faith, in purity."* As a pastor's wife, I must desire to be a good example, and I must embrace the judging eyes of others as an opportunity to influence them for the Lord. Ladies in the church will "take their cues" from the pastor's wife. She will often set the tone and the standard in the church. If I don't make time for soulwinning, the ladies will think it is not important. If I stay home from church because I have a headache, they will stay home when they get a headache. If my children run wild at the church, their children will run wild, too. Get the idea?

God's requirements for godly wives are basically covered in the admonitions given to all Christian women (Titus 2:3–5; 1 Timothy 3:11; 1 Peter 3:1–4; Ephesians 5:21–25; Proverbs 31). The Bible has a wealth of information and instruction that we can apply to our lives. I truly believe that if we would heed God's commands and be controlled by the Holy Spirit, we would be perfect wives! Failing to be "perfect" is no reason to quit striving for the goal.

Defining a godly wife? That's easy! Becoming a godly wife— now that's a tougher task! So, let's move on to the next chapter and take a closer look at becoming a godly Christian woman.

*The aged women likewise, that they be in behaviour as becometh holiness, not false accusers, not given to much wine, teachers of good things; That they may teach the young women to be sober, to love their husbands, to love their children, To be discreet, chaste, keepers at home, good, obedient to their own husbands, that the word of God be not blasphemed.—*TITUS 2:3–5

CHAPTER TWO

Becoming a Godly Woman

*N*ow that we have clarified (and hopefully simplified!) the definition of a godly wife, let's examine *God's* definition of a godly *woman.* Before God called you to fulfill the *role* of a wife, He called you to develop a *relationship* with Him. Who you *are* as a woman of God is more important than what you *do* as a wife. What attributes does God use to define a godly woman? Have you looked into the mirror of His Word recently to check for any areas of improvement in *your* walk with Him? An intimate relationship with God is the foundation of an effective life and ministry and is the only means of possessing the qualities He desires for us to have (Galatians 5:22–23).

So, consider this chapter a checklist—a personal standard for your own life, family, heart, and walk with God. I hope you will refer to it often, review the questions, and allow the Holy Spirit to challenge and stir you in your Christian life.

Biblical Principles

Paul, in his letter to Titus, gives a comprehensive (and convicting) definition of a godly woman. Let me encourage you to study these qualities found in Titus 2 and seek to cultivate them in your own life.

> *The aged women likewise, that they be in behaviour as becometh holiness, not false accusers, not given to much wine, teachers of good things; That they may teach the young women to be sober, to love their husbands, to love their children, to be discreet, chaste, keepers at home, good, obedient to their own husbands, that the word of God be not blasphemed.*—TITUS 2:3–5

Wise

The first God-given attribute of the mature Christian woman is wisdom. The word *sober* in Titus 2:4 means, "stable, sensible, or *wise.*" Wisdom is applying the truth and knowledge of God to everyday life. It is obtained by understanding the fear of the Lord and applying our hearts to know His Word. We must recognize that true wisdom only comes from having a close relationship with the Lord—there is no other way to possess it.

The Bible says in Proverbs 2:4 to seek for wisdom as we would search for silver or hidden treasures. As a teenager, I lived in San Jose, California, and each year the local newspaper sponsored a treasure hunt. The newspaper staff would hide a little tube somewhere in the valley, and each day they would publish a clue on the front page of the paper as to its location. The first person to find the tube won a cash prize!

One year, my mom and I decided that we would look for that treasure. We diligently searched the San Jose countryside every day and spent many hours that summer looking for the mysterious tube. Honestly, after all the time and effort we exerted, we never even came close to finding that treasure!

Many of us spend our lives looking for "things" of no eternal value—like that hidden tube! Maybe your "tube" is popularity, prestige, or possessions. How much more profitable and rewarding it is to search the Scripture for the invaluable truths contained therein!

The wisdom of God is the greatest treasure a person can discover. And there is good news! It's not just given to the first one who claims it! Wisdom can be found by all who seek after her.

> *If any of you lack wisdom, let him ask of God, that giveth to all men liberally, and upbraideth not; and it shall be given him.*
> —JAMES 1:5

Loving

The second command given in this passage is to love your husband and children. We will study this topic in greater detail in the following pages, but before we continue, I'd like to remind you of the following truth: There are many women who can carry out work or duties in the church, but only *you* can be the wife of your husband and the mother of his children. Other than your walk with the Lord, nothing should be more important to you than faithfully and unconditionally loving your family. The church can enlist another nursery director, singer, teacher, or secretary, but your family cannot enlist another wife or mother. Your family is your first ministry and calling in life.

Discreet

The third quality of a godly woman is discretion. Discretion means, "to show prudence, modesty, and wise self-restraint; to walk circumspectly." A discreet woman is *self-controlled* instead of *self-centered*. She is not in bondage to her impulses, passions, and desires, and she does not indulge in every craving of the flesh. A discreet Christian woman does not draw attention to herself, but points the attention to the Lord.

Pure

It has been said that in Paul's day, the culture was noted for its immorality. I believe our culture today is also very promiscuous. God wants us, as women, to be *chaste* or *pure*. Our testimony should be clean, morally pure, set apart, and innocent. This does not happen by chance. It is by our choice and by God's enabling and grace.

Elizabeth George, in her book, *A Woman's High Calling,* gives these practical ways to purify our lives and honor the Lord:

> Acknowledge God's standard.
> Assume God's standard as your standard.
> Admit any and all sin against God's standard.
> Avoid compromising situations.
> Avoid compromising people.
> Ask for accountability.
> Acknowledge the consequences impurity reaps.
> Aspire to a life of obedience—a holy life has a voice![2]

Domesticated

One of my favorite pastimes is walking through model homes to get ideas and look at decorations. I like the "feeling" I get when I walk into those homes. Everything smells new and looks perfect. Nothing is broken (yet). The decorations are "in style," and the rooms are clean. I even walked in one model home recently that had cookies baking in the oven so the enticing aroma would make us feel "at home"! May I remind you though, that no one lives in a model home! So, maybe your house doesn't always look perfect because you have precious people who actually live in it, but it *should* be presentable, orderly, and well-kept.

The biblical term *keepers at home* found in Titus 2:5 is the fine art, or should I say, the lost art, of homemaking. When a woman begins to believe the world's philosophy that a "keeper at home" lacks the importance, skill, or intelligence of an outside corporation, she may begin to replace an eternally rewarding *position* for a temporal and inferior *occupation*. Don't buy into the world's lie that keeping your home is a lower calling in life!

Good

Our next responsibility and purpose is to be *good*. We often lecture our children on the importance of "being good." ("Be good when we go into this restaurant." "You'd better be good at Johnny's house." "Your Sunday school teacher had better tell me that you were good in class today!") Yet, here in the Scripture, God is commanding *us* to "be good"!

The dictionary defines *good* as "being positive or desirable in nature." John Wesley defined *good* from Titus 2 as "being well tempered, soft, and obliging." I like his definition. Are you well tempered? Do people desire to be around you? Are you allowing the Holy Spirit to produce goodness in your life?

> *For we are his workmanship, created in Christ Jesus unto good works, which God hath before ordained that we should walk in them.*—EPHESIANS 2:10

Obedient

Not only are you to love your husband, you are also to obey him. This is not a popular subject in our society, yet the Bible commands wives to obey and reverence their husbands.

God appointed the man to be the leader in the home. This does not mean that you should be passive and that your husband is allowed to walk all over you. It does mean, however, that you should respectfully and humbly submit to his God-given authority. You should obey him, not because he always deserves it, but because God has commanded it. God deserves it.

It has often been said that there is safety in submission! You are not accountable for the way you lead your home, but for how you follow the leadership in your life! How are you growing in the areas of respect and submission in your marriage? Do you

privately or publicly ridicule your husband's faults? Do you have
a good spirit about his decisions? Do you submit to his decisions
even when you disagree? Do you respectfully state your opinions
when they differ? Learn to appreciate your husband's leadership in
the home and express that appreciation to him regularly!

Practical Checklist

I like to make lists. (I like completing and checking them off even
better!) So, now that we've laid the biblical foundation of the
characteristics of a godly woman, let's take these qualities and form
a personal evaluation list. What do these character traits look like
in the context of the different relationships of our lives? How can
we practically apply these principles?

Take time to review the following lists: Are you fulfilling
God's requirements for a Christian woman? Are there some areas
you could not "check off"? Remember this is just a guideline, and
you cannot truly exhibit these traits without the enabling and
empowerment of God's Holy Spirit. Ask Him to grow you in the
following areas.

Personal Life
Your Relationship with the Lord. Before you can begin to develop
a Christ-honoring relationship with your church or family, you
must establish and maintain a meaningful love relationship with
the Lord. You must be cultivating spiritual growth daily and
allowing Christ to work in your heart. How can you be a godly
helpmeet to your husband if you are not truly seeking the One
whom your husband serves? Here is a personal checklist for your
walk with God:

- ❏ I am walking daily with the Lord in Bible reading and prayer.

- ❏ I am surrendering my will to God's on a daily basis.

- ❏ I am keeping short accounts with God by confessing known sin.

❑   I am striving to conform my life to the image of Christ.

That I may know him, and the power of his resurrection, and the fellowship of his sufferings, being made conformable unto his death.—PHILIPPIANS 3:10

Your Personal Life. The godly woman is discreet, according to Titus 2. Discretion is a matter of practicing self-control and godly discipline, which develop character and increase effectiveness for the Lord. It involves curbing your own desires, impulses, and opinions for the sake of your testimony (and the Gospel's). A woman of discretion practices self-denial. Matthew 16:24 says, *"Then said Jesus unto his disciples, If any man will come after me, let him deny himself, and take up his cross, and follow me."*

The Bible also tells us to be chaste (clean, innocent, modest, morally pure, and consecrated). To be chaste is a condition of the heart—who I *am*, not what I *do*. Are the following statements true of your personal life?

❑   I exercise control in my actions, attitudes, and appetites.

❑   I am particular about what I read and watch on TV.

❑   I dress in a fashion that pleases the Lord and my husband.

❑   I maintain a healthy, balanced lifestyle in diet and exercise.

❑   I refrain from negative thinking and talking.

❑   I refrain from fantasizing about things that displease God.

But I keep under my body, and bring it into subjection: lest that by any means, when I have preached to others, I myself should be a castaway.—1 CORINTHIANS 9:27

Home Life
Your Relationship with Your Husband. Unconditional love is intentionally cultivated. This kind of love is vastly different from the romantic, emotional love that often initially attracts you to a

person and creates in you a desire for marriage. Are you denying yourself in deference to your husband's needs? Ask God to search your heart in these areas:

❑   I am striving to meet his physical needs.

❑   I am striving to meet his emotional needs.

❑   I am striving to meet his recreational needs.

❑   I am fulfilling my role as a helpmeet.

❑   I am supporting him in his calling.

❑   I do not go to bed with anger or bitterness in my heart.

❑   I do my best to be physically attractive and pleasing to him.

And the LORD God said, It is not good that the man should be alone; I will make him an help meet for him.—GENESIS 2:18

Your Relationship with Your Children. Paul wrote to Timothy to honor widows who were *"well reported of for good works; if she have brought up children, if she have lodged strangers, if she have washed the saints' feet, if she have relieved the afflicted, if she have diligently followed every good work"* (1 Timothy 5:10).

Your children may have several teachers or godly Christians in their lives, but you are their only mother. You are the only person who can bring them up in the nurture and admonition of the Lord on a daily basis, and you are commanded by God to provide these needs in their lives. Don't neglect the high calling of motherhood in exchange for your position in the ministry. How are you doing in these areas?

❑   I delight in my high calling as a godly mother.

❑   I find joy in raising my children.

❑   I find fulfillment in meeting their needs.

❑   I am committed to the Lord in raising children for His glory.

Childrearing is the art of choosing to selflessly love and shape the life of a child. A wise mother realizes that loving her children will require a sacrificial investment of time, discipline, and attention. A mother who loves her children with this type of biblical love will gladly give herself to the task of teaching principles and skills that will equip them to live godly and productive lives. She understands that well-behaved children do not "just happen," and she accepts the time-consuming responsibility of nurturing them in the Word of God.

❑ I am regularly teaching them to love the Lord by my words.

❑ I am regularly teaching them to love the Lord by my actions.

❑ I am training them in life skills and personal discipline habits.

❑ I am keeping my temper under control.

❑ I am disciplining them according to scriptural methods.

❑ I am modeling a life of surrender and submission.

❑ I am creating happy memories and joyful family time.

Train up a child in the way he should go: and when he is old, he will not depart from it.—PROVERBS 22:6

Your Care of the Home. In our society, homemaking has been looked down upon as old-fashioned and legalistic. In reality, it is one of the most important jobs in the world. A godly homemaker is really a domestic engineer. She is the guardian of the home and takes pride in guiding and caring for her household.

Managing the home doesn't always come naturally or easily; it takes time, energy, and creativity. Yet, our homes should be a comfortable, happy, and secure place.

Do you love making your house a home? Do you love meeting the needs of your family? Consider these points:

❑ I prepare balanced and nutritious meals faithfully.

❑   I keep the house decent and in order.

❑   I am a good steward when purchasing groceries, etc.

❑   I plan ahead, budget, and look for sales.

❑   I seek to provide peace and harmony in the home.

That they may teach the young women to be sober, to love their husbands, to love their children, to be discreet, chaste, keepers at home, good, obedient to their own husbands, that the word of God be not blasphemed.—TITUS 2:4–5

Ministry Life

One of the simple exhortations to women in Titus 2:5 is to be *good* or *virtuous*. It is important for those in the ministry to possess virtue. What are some areas that will help you be a virtuous Christian servant?

Supporting Your Husband's Work. When you married your husband, you accepted his life's call. Your husband was trusting you to be a help and support as he fulfilled God's calling in his life. Do you encourage and stand by him in this work? Is he a better servant of God because of your love and ministry in his life? God placed you in his life to complete this call. Consider this list as you ask the Lord to help you fully support your husband's ministry:

❑   I am his greatest encourager and cheerleader.

❑   I provide a listening ear and a helping hand at all times.

❑   I make his needs my first priority throughout the day.

❑   I use my words to uplift, edify, and encourage him.

❑   I respond to God through my husband's preaching.

❑   I am flexible with ministry demands.

The heart of her husband doth safely trust in her, so that he shall have no need of spoil.—PROVERBS 31:11

Exercising Faith. The Bible says that *"whatsoever is not of faith is sin"* (Romans 14:23). Are you giving to God by faith? Are you expecting God to meet your needs even when circumstances seem impossible? Other ladies will be watching you. Do they see a woman who is trusting in God on a daily basis? Consider the following statements:

❏   I support my husband's desire to practice sacrificial giving.

❏   I maintain a positive spirit during difficult circumstances.

❏   I set an example of faith in God for other ladies to follow.

❏   I choose to be content with what God has given to me.

Remembering without ceasing your work of faith, and labour of love, and patience of hope in our Lord Jesus Christ, in the sight of God and our Father.—1 THESSALONIANS 1:3

Maintaining a Good Testimony. You have the ability to ruin your husband's reputation and even his ministry. Are you setting a pattern of good works? Could other women strive to emulate your good example?

❏   I am consistent in my habits, attitudes, and actions.

❏   I avoid gossip and conversations that tear down other people.

❏   I build up my husband and his ministry in public.

❏   I build up my husband and his ministry in private.

❏   I avoid the appearance of evil.

❏   I willingly embrace standards of modesty to honor Christ.

❏   I willingly embrace other standards to honor Christ.

In all things shewing thyself a pattern of good works: in doctrine shewing uncorruptness, gravity, sincerity.—TITUS 2:7

Soulwinning. Sometimes it is difficult to juggle family responsibilities with the weekly soulwinning schedule, but the Bible does command us to reach others with the Gospel. It is important to make soulwinning a priority in your life, even if it means saying no to other activities or events. It is vital to model a soulwinner's heart before your children and your church family. Do you pass this test?

- ❑   I go soulwinning faithfully every week.

- ❑   I carry tracts and consistently pass them out to people I meet.

- ❑   I take my children out doorknocking.

- ❑   I am praying for opportunities to win others to Christ.

The fruit of the righteous is a tree of life; and he that winneth souls is wise.—PROVERBS 11:30

Discipling New Christians. Other ladies are watching you, whether or not you actually teach a Sunday school class or conduct a Bible study. Your life will constantly be an example to your new members, as well as the other wives and mothers in the church. You are constantly discipling others by your very life. What does your life teach them about Spirit-filled conduct? Does your character set a precedent before you ever set foot in a classroom or teach with your words? Prayerfully examine your heart in this light:

- ❑   I am ready to disciple new Christians at the altar each service.

- ❑   I am prepared to counsel others with appropriate Bible verses.

- ❑   I am prepared to use Scripture to encourage others.

- ❑   I am learning truths in my personal walk to share with others.

- ❑   I creatively present Bible truths in my Sunday school class.

The aged women likewise, that they be in behaviour as becometh holiness, not false accusers, not given to much wine, teachers of good things.—TITUS 2:3

Edifying Others. God has given every one of us unique abilities and gifts. You may not be able to sing a solo or accompany the song leader on the piano, but can you encourage a widow or serve in the nursery? Ask the Lord to show you your gifts and how you can use them to be a blessing to others. Don't bemoan what you cannot do; embrace what you can do with a happy heart. Be who God created you to be!

❏ I look for ways to encourage and be a blessing to others.

❏ I use the gifts God has given me to the best of my ability.

❏ I am content with my God-given gifts.

❏ I practice giving to others.

But unto every one of us is given grace according to the measure of the gift of Christ.—EPHESIANS 4:7

Encouraging the Saints. While your children are small, your ability to participate in every activity may be limited. Don't let this keep you from encouraging others. You can have a special ministry of encouragement, whether that is baking cookies for a friend or making a phone call to a lonely widow. Do you accept any limitations you may have and still look for creative ways to encourage others each week? Here's a good checklist:

❏ I am conscious of those who are discouraged or lonely.

❏ I respond to discouraged people as soon as possible.

❏ I exercise the gift of encouragement on a daily basis.

❏ I include my children in encouraging others.

❏ I regularly reach out to those who are suffering.

❑   I seek to encourage more than to be encouraged.

For God is not unrighteous to forget your work and labour of love, which ye have shewed toward his name, in that ye have ministered to the saints, and do minister.—Hebrews 6:10

Providing for the Needs of Others. When you hear that another brother or sister in Christ has a need, how do you respond? You may feel overwhelmed by your own financial pressures, but God wants you to exercise faith in this area of giving. He promises to supply all of your needs as you help meet the needs of others.

❑   I quickly respond when a need is brought to my attention.

❑   I give to others willingly, trusting God to supply my needs.

❑   I bring others' burdens before the Lord in prayer.

If a brother or sister be naked, and destitute of daily food, And one of you say unto them, Depart in peace, be ye warmed and filled; notwithstanding ye give them not those things which are needful to the body; what doth it profit? Even so faith, if it hath not works, is dead, being alone.—James 2:15–17

Relieving the Afflicted. It is easy to become so focused on the immediate needs of your family that you neglect or fail to notice those who are hurting. It doesn't take talent or ability to give comfort to others. Often a kind word or a note of encouragement is sufficient in brightening up someone's day. How are you doing in these areas?

❑   I regularly write notes of encouragement or sympathy.

❑   I provide a meal or childcare for families in need.

❑   I am attentive to those who are struggling or hurting.

❑   I respond to the Holy Spirit's promptings to reach out.

Well reported of for good works; if she have brought up children,
if she have lodged strangers, if she have washed the saints' feet,
if she have relieved the afflicted, if she have diligently followed
every good work.—1 TIMOTHY 5:10

Wow! That's quite a checklist! Are you feeling overwhelmed? Don't be discouraged, and remember—this is just a guide! God expects from the pastor's wife the same attributes He expects from other godly women in the church. He is not asking you to be or do the impossible. He's not expecting you to be perfect in every way or highly talented (like those examples that were mentioned earlier in the book). You should actually be encouraged and relieved when you consider that *God* will *develop* these traits within you—all you have to do is yield to Him!

Through Christ's strength, you can be a godly wife to your husband! You can strengthen and encourage him as he fulfills God's calling in his life! By fulfilling your role faithfully, you can greatly multiply his influence and ministry. Yes, there will be times of trials and heartache. You will feel inadequate, but you will also reap great blessings as you experience the rewards of being a support and helpmeet to the man of God!

No one knows your husband better than you do, and the truth is, no one's respect, admiration, support, or encouragement will mean more to him than yours! Your husband is probably only too aware of his inadequacies and faults—and he knows you are too! When you choose to love, support, and encourage him, it means more than words can describe. No one can take his heart where you can! So, take it there!

If you are a pastor's wife, God has given you a pastor and a husband all in one package. Now, ask Him to enable you to be the godly woman your husband needs, and watch Him do great things through you together.

CHAPTER THREE

Preparing for Ministry

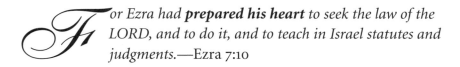

*or Ezra had **prepared his heart** to seek the law of the LORD, and to do it, and to teach in Israel statutes and judgments.—Ezra 7:10*

Emotional Preparation

When our children turn four years old, we usually start to prepare them for kindergarten. We tell them all about the school day, and let them know what to expect. We sometimes even teach them their ABC's in an effort to give them a head start! By the time August rolls around, Staples runs their "Back to School" commercial—the one where the father takes his two children to the store to buy all their school supplies. You hear "It's the Most Wonderful Time of the Year" playing over the loudspeakers, and you see the dad happily kicking his heels together. (Obviously, his children are not starting kindergarten!)

This is the time of year when we take our kindergartners-to-be shopping for school clothes and school supplies. We buy their lunch foods, lunch boxes, and backpacks. The night before school starts, we give them a nice bath and lay out all their clothes.

Kindergarten is a new experience for kids! It's often an exciting and somewhat scary time for them. That is why we put forth our best effort as parents to ease the fear of starting this new era of life. We want them to be ready and prepared for an enjoyable first day of school!

If you are a new pastor's wife or a veteran pastor's wife, you can probably relate to these same emotions of excitement, nervousness, and fear! Entering the ministry or serving in the ministry can often feel overwhelming and frightening. Frankly, these feelings still arise every time God brings a new experience into my life. It is during these times that I remember: God wants to prepare me in every area of my life, including my emotions! Just as a concerned parent thoroughly prepares a child for the first day of school, my Heavenly Father desires to "throughly furnish" me unto *all* good works! My fears are calmed and my trust in Him is restored as I prepare my heart through prayer and reading His Word.

Educational Preparation

When my husband and I were expecting our first child, we decided to prepare ourselves by taking Lamaze classes. We eagerly attended our first meeting, where we were introduced to all the other parents-to-be. We were then instructed how to take care of mom and baby during the pregnancy. You know—get plenty of rest and exercise (I still can't figure out "plenty of rest and exercise;" it sounds like an oxymoron to me!), eat right, avoid all the bad stuff, and take your vitamins. All of this information was great, except for the fact that I had just begun my last month of pregnancy!

The very next week (thinking I was going into labor), I checked into the hospital's maternity ward only to discover I was having a kidney stone! We never did finish our Lamaze classes, and a few weeks later, without the help of Lamaze, we were parents of a precious baby girl!

Maybe that's how you feel about your ministry preparation! Many pastors' wives did not have an opportunity to prepare for ministry by attending Bible college. Others, like me, went to Bible college but never had a class on being a pastor's wife. Praise the Lord that lack of "professional" training does not disqualify us from being a pastors' wives any more than not having Lamaze classes disqualified me from having a baby.

Whether or not you have had the "professional" training to be a pastor's wife, I hope you will join me in doing everything you can to continually prepare and educate yourself for the position into which God has placed you.

Spiritual Preparation

I enjoy studying the life of Esther. She was an orphaned Jew who prepared herself for one full year before God allowed her to become queen. Once she was queen, she fasted in preparation for her meeting with the king to ask for deliverance of her people. In both instances, I believe God used Esther's preparation to bring about His will.

Just as Esther prepared herself for the task God had given her, so we ought to prepare and continue preparing for the work of the ministry that God has given us. The simple fact is, we have much to learn about the Lord and His work. God will enable us, strengthen us, and bless us as we give ourselves to preparing for His call.

Throughout the Old Testament we see God's army *preparing* for battle. We are in a battle as well—a spiritual battle. The devil will attack us, discourage us, and do everything in his power to defeat us. The devil will use our insecurities to cause us to question our…

> education,
> background,
> Bible knowledge,
> talent,
> personality, or
> fears of failure.

Friend, the best way to fight the devil is to be prepared for his attacks! None of the things listed above are reasons to quit, but they are reasons to prepare and to give ourselves to the task of growing in God's grace.

Practical Preparation

I realize that every Christian woman is different. We all have different responsibilities, gifts, personalities, and talents. Yet, I believe there are ways to prepare for the personalized tasks that God has waiting for us in the ministry. The more we prepare, the less fear, anxiety, and frustration we will experience as we serve Christ.

Let me encourage you to begin a personal journey of preparation. Decide today that you will begin seeking and developing the tools and skills that God desires to give you. Every area of preparation takes time and sacrifice, but the rewards are plentiful. You will bless your husband, encourage his ministry, increase his effectiveness, and honor the Lord as you give yourself to growing in your role.

Let's examine a few practical ways that you can prepare your heart and life for your unique responsibilities. In the following pages, I encourage you to focus on the following:

+ Develop a close walk with the Lord.

- Observe godly women in other leadership roles.
- Continue training.
- Set up a regular reading program.
- Establish a filing system.
- Keep a journal.
- Practice good stewardship.

Develop a Close Walk with the Lord

I am convinced the most important way we can prepare for ministry or any other area of our Christian life is to develop a close walk with God! This is the baseline of ministry. This is where it all begins. It would be impossible to impact and strengthen others in their walks with the Lord if we are not maintaining a close relationship with Him personally.

Before Ezra taught the people, he *"prepared his heart to seek the law of the LORD"* (Ezra 7:10). My time with the Lord in prayer and reading His Word gives me strength and wisdom to minister to others. I encourage you to become a student of the Bible. Discover where to find answers, so you can be prepared to meet needs and answer questions. First Peter 3:15 says, *"But sanctify the Lord God in your hearts: and be ready always to give an answer to every man that asketh you a reason of the hope that is in you with meekness and fear."* (Keep in mind that it is okay to say, "I don't know, but I will find out," and then make sure you do!)

Years ago, my husband was invited to preach at a teen camp in New England. I had not been to that part of the country before, so we thought it would be fun to leave a little early and to do some sightseeing together. Our first destination was the Statue of Liberty. Hearing that the traffic and parking were very difficult in New York, we decided to take the subway into the city. We purchased our tokens, looked at the map, and took our first ride on the subway. It was all very exciting, except for one minor detail. This particular train did not go directly to the Statue of Liberty. We had to change trains along the way—and the second train was noticeably different from the first! It was covered with horrible graffiti and packed with questionable characters. Worst of all, it did not take us to the Statue of Liberty! It took us to the Bronx—not good. I'll never forget the fear that crept into my heart as we stepped off that train. My first instinct was to hold my husband's arm tighter and to walk as closely to him as possible. I remember trying to "walk as one" with my husband in that scary environment.

What is your instinctive response to feeling inadequate and fearful about your ministry position? I pray that it is to cling more tightly to the Lord's hand and to walk more closely with Him. Are you "walking as one" with the Lord, just as I tried to do with my husband that day?

When the train doors of my life open up, and I find myself walking into new and fearful areas of life and ministry, I just hold on a little tighter to and walk a little closer with the Lord. He will give the needed strength to go on in His will.

Observe Godly Women in Other Leadership Roles

I was born in Kansas City, Missouri, and I have adopted their state motto, "The Show Me State," as my own. I am a "show me" type of person. I learn best when I am shown how to do something. In addition to this, I'm a "people-watcher." Leave me in the middle of a busy airport, and I can entertain myself for hours. When you put these two qualities together, they make for some great learning experiences!

Since I did not grow up in a preacher's home or around a pastor's wife, I didn't have a clue what it meant to be a good pastor's wife. So, I began to watch and glean from the lives of godly women. God revealed good character traits in these women that I asked Him to incorporate into my own life.

My first role model was my mother-in-law, who was also the wife of my first pastor. She would warmly greet a visiting lady at the front of the church, lovingly put her arm around her, and escort her to a counseling room where she would tell her of

Christ. She taught me that there was great joy in serving. Whether working on a bus route, teaching a Sunday school class, discipling a new Christian, or cleaning the church, she consistently served the Lord with gladness.

As a Bible college student, I followed the examples of my Sunday school teachers, who opened their homes to the singles every Sunday night for fellowship and food. And, as a young pastor's wife, I purposefully noticed the mannerisms, attitudes, and actions of ladies such as Mrs. Lee Roberson, who took notes of all her husband's messages—messages she had heard many times before.

When the Lord gives me the opportunity to be with godly women, especially women who have walked with the Lord for many years, I purpose to make our time together a learning experience. I ask questions, listen to answers, and strive to apply what I hear to specific areas of my own life. I cherish the memories and treasure the lessons I've learned from so many godly women.

Continue Training

My oldest sister is a runner. She has competed in hundreds of marathons, and it seems that every time I talk to her, she is preparing for another race. If there is one thing I've noticed about her training, it is that she doesn't wait until the day before competing to begin conditioning. In fact, her training never stops! (I get tired just thinking about her!)

I learned early in the ministry that I must be a life-long student. Even after twenty-five years of service to the Lord, I know I still have so much to learn. I want to continue growing and preparing for the next task God has waiting for me. I realize that my training never really stops—God desires that I be constantly preparing for the next step of the journey.

I encourage you to become a life-long student as well. Decide to embark on an unending journey to learn, discover, and grow in God's grace.

Ask God to reveal areas in your life that need improvement, and ask Him to provide opportunities and tools that would better equip you for His use. Perhaps you could attend a Christ-honoring conference or seminar. (Now that my children are older, I enjoy occasionally traveling with my husband when he goes to a conference. Not only is this extra time with him, but it's also a time to learn and increase my effectiveness.) You may enjoy reading, so keep your eyes open for informative articles and book sales. Our public library has a sale twice a year that allows you to buy a bag of books for $1. Take advantage of opportunities such as this.

There are many ways to continue training, depending on what is available to you. Consider this short list of ideas:

- Take a class in speedreading.
- Attend a time-management seminar.
- Start instrument or voice lessons.
- Learn sign language.
- Take a speech class.
- Read books about biblical counseling.
- Study creative writing.
- Take a class on CPR.
- Order the ladies' sessions CDs from a conference.

Set Up a Regular Reading Program

We've all heard the adage "readers are leaders," but in today's culture, reading has taken the back seat to television, videos, video games, and the internet! It is vital that you fall in love with the lost art of reading.

Reading sharpens the mind, challenges us in our daily walk, increases our vocabulary, and informs us as growing children of God. The first and most important book we should read is, of course, the Bible. Amy Carmichael said, "Never let good books take the place of the Bible. Drink from the Well, not from the streams that flow from the Well." Reading the Bible allows us to grow in our faith and understand the heart and mind of God. Second, we should read books that shed light on areas of our Christian growth and development. Third, we should read biographies of men and women who have been used of God in the past.

Remember, we must use godly discernment when we read! There is a Japanese proverb that says, "If you believe everything you read, you better not read." (Add to that statement, "…anything but the Bible," of course!) One author wrote, "Books, like friends, should be few and well-chosen." I think that's pretty good advice!

If you're not an avid reader, let me encourage you to start slowly and to set a goal to read a certain number of books in the next twelve months. My husband and I spend one week together every year for the sole purpose of strengthening our marriage. We get away, we talk, and we read books that will help us grow spiritually and that will build our marriage as well. It is a time that we both treasure and a time that has proven invaluable for spiritual growth and preparation in both of our lives.

Establish a Filing System

Another way to prepare for what may lie ahead in ministry is to have a good filing system. If you're like me, you're always on the lookout for lesson truths, ideas for ladies' activities, and easy recipes. I have established a filing system that now contains a wealth of information, and it has been said that "information is power if you can find it when you need it!" My filing system allows me to approach an activity or event with less anxiety, knowing the information I need to get started is exactly where it should be.

To start your filing system, ask the Lord to help you intuitively look for fresh ideas, teaching thoughts, and ministry helps in every circumstance. You'll be surprised how the Lord will provide ideas when you least expect them. (I've found great ideas from looking at greeting cards, playing games with my family, or reading magazines or even cookbooks!) When an idea comes to mind, write it down immediately, and then file it as soon as possible.

Your filing system should be set up in a way that will allow for quick and easy retrieval (alphabetically, topically, etc.), and can contain topics such as illustrations, ladies' retreat themes, Sunday school lessons, devotionals, games, shower ideas (baby and bridal), and more! It will be an invaluable resource as you prepare for future ministry opportunities.

Keep a Journal

"It's hard for me to keep a diary because it seems to me that I— nor for that matter—anyone else would ever be interested in the secrets of a thirteen-year-old school girl."

Those words were penned by Anne Frank in 1942, and how wrong she was! She, because of her diary, became a symbol for Jews who lost their lives during World War II.

I encourage you to keep a journal, a scrapbook, or some record of your life, your growth, and your journey with the Lord. Now, I'll be the first to admit that our journals will probably never be turned into books or movies, but they will leave a legacy for those who follow behind us. Journals also serve as personal memorials in our own lives. They often provide encouragement in times of uncertainty and joy in times of reminiscing as we meditate on the work and goodness of God in our lives.

From her statement above, we see how Anne Frank thought the little things of her life didn't matter. But the "small stuff" *is* everything—it is what our stories are made of. No blessing from

God or special event allowed by Him is too small to record for ourselves and for those who come after us.

Perhaps you can begin now by simply keeping a blessing book. Someone said we often write our blessings in the sand and our burdens in cement. Let's break out of the mold of the typical and decide to keep a record of how God has blessed us. Over the years, the blessings I have recorded have helped me remember God's faithfulness in the past. They remind me that He will prove Himself to be faithful again and that He will never fail me. Read through your journal or blessing book often and let God strengthen your heart through those pages.

If there is one area of my life that I regret at this point, it is that I did not journal more consistently and take more pictures in years past. I used to say, "I will never forget that," and then I did! It seems impossible to remember all the events of your life accurately, so be sure to record significant events and important seasons of growth.

It is never too late to start keeping a journal, no matter what your age or background—so start today! Years from now, you'll be very glad you did.

Practice Good Stewardship

You may be wondering how practicing good stewardship will help prepare you for ministry and leadership. Well, perhaps this story will help explain what I mean.

One of the "hidden" blessings we enjoyed when coming to Lancaster Baptist was that we did not have any debt. Since our monthly payments were low, we were free to go where God wanted us to go. We were not a burden to the church, and we didn't have to look for higher paying opportunities. If we had been in debt in 1986, that may have been a hindrance to our following the Lord and launching out by faith.

Another blessing came a few months after moving to Lancaster. Prior to our move, we had saved several thousand dollars in hopes that someday the Lord would allow us to purchase a home. But coming to Lancaster required that we put all that money into moving, renovating the church, and starting the ministry. So we were back to square one when it came to saving for a home—and we were taking a church that offered no salary.

Not long after we arrived in town, some long-time friends that we hadn't seen in a while came to visit. The weather was extremely hot that day, and our little duplex didn't have air conditioning. Walking into our home that afternoon was like walking into a sauna. On top of that, we lived in a very bad part of town—the kind of place where no one really wants to spend a lot of time.

For this reason, we weren't surprised when our guests immediately suggested that we all take a drive and see the area. The car had great air conditioning—which made their idea all the more attractive!

As we were driving, we passed by a new home development with a sign that said, "Only One House Left." Suddenly our friend turned the car and said he wanted to take a look at that house. We assumed he was interested in possibly making an investment purchase.

A few moments later, we had walked through the house and our friend began talking to the real estate agent. He asked how much money they needed down on the house. We were hoping that he would buy the house and then allow us to rent it from him.

When the agent told us the down payment amount, it was the exact amount that we had depleted from our savings when we moved to Lancaster. In that moment, our friend took out his checkbook and gave the agent the down payment.

I cannot describe to you the joy and emotion that filled our hearts that day when our friends told the agent that this home would be in our name and that the down payment was their gift to us. We were amazed and grateful.

The lending agent proceeded to fill out the loan information and soon asked my husband for his salary. He simply said, "It is whatever God provides." She laughed. But, when she realized he wasn't joking, she called her boss.

One of the questions he asked during that phone call was how much debt we had. Because we didn't have any, her boss said, "I don't know why I am saying this, but go ahead with the loan."

The story doesn't end there! At that point our friend said, "I want them to live in this house immediately and to live here rent-free until the escrow closes."

The realtor said that this would never happen, but she called her boss once again. A few moments later he had approved the request. It was a miracle! We lived in that new home for almost four months—rent-free. We learned a huge lesson that day. When we are living by faith and staying out of debt, God is able to do abundantly more than we can ask or think.

Wise stewardship definitely has its rewards!

Ministry is exciting, and we never know what God has in store for us next. Lord Baden Powell was the originator of the Scout motto: "Be Prepared." Someone once asked him, "Be prepared for what?" to which Lord Baden Powell replied, "Be prepared for *everything*." Wherever we find ourselves in ministry, we must always be preparing for tomorrow. Keep growing in your walk with the Lord. Observe other godly women. Continue training. Read as often as you can. Develop a good filing system. Maintain a journal and a blessing book. Be a wise steward.

H. Jackson Brown, Jr., author of *Life's Little Instruction Book*, said, "The best preparation for tomorrow is doing your best today!" So, start now! Begin preparing for a future of growth and reward as you live out God's plan for your life.

CHAPTER FOUR

How Satan Wants To Destroy Your Ministry

*I*n one of our recent staff meetings, a guest speaker gave the following statistic: Only twenty percent of the people who begin in the ministry actually *finish* in the ministry. As I sat there, I began to think of many Bible college classmates who are no longer serving the Lord. I realized in that moment, that the devil would like nothing more than to destroy my ministry and my husband's calling as pastor.

Sadly, this statistic has been followed by more evidence that the ministry is under greater attack now than at any other time in the history of the church. Consider these statistics:

Pastors
- Fifteen hundred pastors leave the ministry each month due to moral failure, spiritual burnout, or contention in their churches.
- Four thousand new churches begin each year, but over seven thousand churches close.

- Eighty percent of pastors and eighty-four percent of their spouses feel unqualified and discouraged in their roles.
- Eighty percent of seminary and Bible school graduates who enter the ministry will leave the ministry within the first five years.
- Ninety percent of pastors say the ministry is completely different from what they thought it would be.
- Seventy percent feel God called them to pastoral ministry before their ministry began, but after three years of ministry, only fifty percent still feel called.

Pastors' Wives

- Eighty percent of pastors' wives feel their spouse is overworked.
- Eighty percent of pastors' wives feel left out and unappreciated by the church members.
- Eighty percent of pastors' wives wish their spouse would choose another profession.
- Eighty percent of pastors' wives feel pressured to do things and be something that they are really not in the church.
- Forty-five percent of pastors' wives fear physical, emotional, and spiritual burnout.
- Sixty percent of pastors' wives work outside the home.
- Forty-five percent of pastors' wives say they have no close friends or mentors.
- The majority of pastors' wives surveyed say that the most destructive event that has occurred in their marriage and family was the day they entered ministry.

Pastors' Marriages

- Almost forty percent polled say they have had an extra-marital affair since beginning their ministry.
- Ninety-five percent of pastors do not regularly pray with their spouses.
- Fifty percent of pastors' marriages end in divorce.

Other than just being scary, these statistics show us how intensely the devil is working to destroy the role of the pastor.

He is relentlessly involved in a destructive pursuit against your husband, your family, your marriage, and your ministry! I don't want to be a statistic. I don't ever want to quit on God, and I don't ever want to fall prey to one of Satan's attacks in this spiritual warfare that we call "ministry."

First Corinthians 9:24–27 compares the Christian life to running a race. Verse twenty-four says, *"Know ye not that they which run in a race run all, but one receiveth the prize? So run, that ye may obtain."* I am not a pastor's wife because there was a shortage of things to do with my life. There is a purpose to my race. God has called me to run alongside my husband, and He doesn't want me to quit! Acts 20:24 says, *"But none of these things move me, neither count I my life dear unto myself, so that I might finish my course with joy, and the ministry, which I have received of the Lord Jesus, to testify the gospel of the grace of God."*

Have you ever driven past a church and seen a sign that says "Pastors Bill and Sandy So-and-So"? I have to confess the only time I ever used the name "Pastor Terrie" was while making a hospital visit a long time ago. Our hospital has a rule that you can only visit new mothers if you are the father or the pastor. A dear lady in our church had a baby, and I wanted to go visit her. When security asked me who I was, I knew I wouldn't get in to see her unless I was a pastor! I said, "Oh, I'm Pastor Chappell's wife…." I emphasized *pastor* very loudly, and security let me into the maternity ward. I have to admit that I felt kind of guilty. Fortunately, my husband did not mind. (And that was the only time I ever used the name "pastor"!)

Pastoring is my *husband's* ministry, not mine! But, as his wife, I have the power to ruin that ministry. You have that same power as the wife of a Christian leader. I know it's not "fun" to even entertain this thought, but its truth is so important. God forbid that we, as wives, would hinder or hurt what God desires to do through the leadership of our husbands.

There are two areas where sin can creep in and destroy not only our ministry, but our husband's ministry as well. If we give the devil even a fraction of an inch in any of these areas, he will take our sin so much farther than we want it to go.

Pride

Pride is an attitude of the heart that can eventually destroy the ministry God has given to us. The Bible has a lot to say about this subject. James 4:6 says, *"But he giveth more grace. Wherefore he saith, God resisteth the proud, but giveth grace unto the humble."* Think about that. When pride creeps in, God resists us—even though we are serving Him!

Proverbs 6:16–19 lists the seven things the Lord hates, and the very first thing He talks about is pride. Proverbs 8:13 says, *"The fear of the LORD is to hate evil: pride, and arrogancy, and the evil way, and the froward mouth, do I hate."* Proverbs 13:10 tells us that *"only by pride cometh contention."*

Let me be transparent with you. In times past, when someone would talk about pride, I would be tempted to think, "I'm not really a prideful person." But, as soon as I had these thoughts, the Lord would bring to mind selfish motives or actions. It was as if His Holy Spirit was saying, "Yes, you are. You just don't realize it!" He would remind me of times in my marriage when I didn't get to eat at the restaurant of my choice or of other situations in which I became a little upset over some self-centered issue, like not being able to keep my own schedule. These attitudes are forms of pride.

Pride is not only the "blatant arrogance" that we usually associate with the term. It is more than saying, "I am so good." Pride emerges in many other subtle forms because it is a deceitful sin. In fact, most people don't even realize they are infected with prideful hearts—like the person who is proud of his humility. Remember that book, *Humility, and How I Attained It*?

So, since most of us have hearts that are tainted with pride, what are some indicators to look for in our own lives?

A proud person is easily irritated.
Have you ever been irritated with your husband or your children? Maybe you are annoyed with a church member you have counseled many times or with someone who just has the spiritual gift of "getting on your nerves."

Have you seen that cartoon with the caption that states, "I have one nerve left, and you are on it"? Simply put, expressed irritation is a form of pride.

Sometimes pride involves more than frustration at "not getting to eat at my favorite restaurant." Pride can also be revealed by how we handle the trials that come to our lives. When we think we don't deserve a trial and are annoyed by the inconvenience, we are allowing pride to take hold. In humility, we must remember that God is in control, and He will never give us more than we can handle. He allows the trials so we will continue to humbly rely on Him for the strength and guidance we desperately need.

A proud person accepts God's praise.
Another indication of pride is when we accept praise for things over which we have no control. If someone ever compliments me after a teaching time (I was definitely not born with a gift for public speaking, nor do I "live" for the next speaking opportunity) or a successful event, I always want to be careful to give God the praise. If you receive a compliment on your wonderful cooking or your church solo, remember to deflect the praise back to the Lord. Give Him the glory for the gifts with which He has enabled you.

A proud person will not admit to a mistake.
Pride also evidences itself when we will not admit to making mistakes. I know very few people who would say, "I refuse to acknowledge when I am wrong," yet many of us struggle with

actually admitting it when we are! Sometimes we make mistakes and try to blame them on other circumstances or people. We tend to rationalize or let others think our failure was someone else's fault. Pride hinders us from taking full responsibility for our own mistakes.

A proud person refuses to receive godly counsel.

I have often heard of couples who, after experiencing marital problems or discouragement in ministry, said, "We were just too proud to let anybody know that we had a problem." My husband and I made a promise to each other when we got married. We agreed to be accountable to godly counselors. Together, we decided that if either of us felt like our marriage was suffering, we would not be too embarrassed or proud to seek counsel.

As pastors' wives and mothers, we need more than marriage counseling! We often need guidance in the ministry or advice on raising godly children. Quite honestly, most of my counseling comes from my husband. I trust his walk with God, his wisdom, and his leadership in our home. A long time ago, I decided that I didn't ever want to come to a point where I questioned his leadership or refused to follow his counsel. God gave him to me for that purpose, and He has always blessed me as I follow His appointed leadership in my life.

A proud person is a competitive person.

A competitive spirit is another indicator of pride: "Do I teach as well as she does?" "Do I sing as well as that lady?" "How was my meal at the potluck?" All of these attitudes express a desire to be better than the next person. The problem with this type of thinking is that it keeps you from truly becoming who God designed you to be. God doesn't compare you to someone else. And when you begin comparing and competing with others, you'll always be better than some and worse than others in your own mind. Whether you win or lose in this competitive thought process, you ultimately lose, because God resists this way of thinking.

Second Corinthians 10:12 says, *"For we dare not make ourselves of the number, or compare ourselves with some that commend themselves: but they measuring themselves by themselves, and comparing themselves among themselves, are not wise."* God says we are not wise when we enter into a comparison mentality.

There are two definitions of pride. The first definition is relatively common, and you have probably heard it many times. "Pride is esteeming oneself above other people." The middle letter of the word *pride* is "I"—*I* can do this, and *I* can do that.

Here is the definition that convicted me: "Pride is an attitude of independence from God." We are not usually so bold as to say, "I don't need God anymore," but pride often appears when we say, "I have been soulwinning every week since we have been in the ministry," or "I have never missed a day of devotions since I first learned to read." Maybe you have taught Sunday school for so long that you have begun to rely on your experience and expertise rather than on the Holy Spirit's working. Pride shows up each time we congratulate ourselves in our own hearts or in every situation in which we act apart from God.

The longer you serve in the ministry, the more you must guard your heart from pride. It seems that as the years go by in service to God, we have a greater desire to "pat ourselves on the back." We must continue to rely on the Lord and ask Him to keep His Word fresh and our hearts humble as He continues to mold us into His image.

Psalm 10:4 says, *"The wicked, through the pride of his countenance, will not seek after God: God is not in all his thoughts."* Is God in all of your thoughts? Are you going to Him for wisdom in everything that you need to accomplish today or are you depending on your own strength?

James 4:6 tells us what we need: *"But he giveth more grace. Wherefore he saith, God resisteth the proud, but giveth grace unto the humble."* God's grace at work in our hearts will enable us to genuinely depend on Him and to sincerely deflect all praise to Him for every ministry and family blessing—for we truly can do nothing apart from Him.

Discontentment

Personal Discontent

Discontentment is the second attitude Satan uses to destroy the ministries of Christian women. A spirit of discontent is something many of us struggle with, no matter how long we've been in the ministry. When we are young, we tend to think, "Oh, if I just had this or that, I could really serve the Lord." As we grow older, our thoughts change to, "I have been faithful for so many years, I really deserve different and better things." Whether we *desire* better things or believe we *deserve* better things, God sees both positions as discontentment.

The opposite of contentment is covetousness. We must be careful to not conform to the world's mindset of materialism. On every corner, we see "For Sale" signs and advertisements for bigger and better cars and houses. Meanwhile, your twenty-year-old car may have broken down last week and your house might feel too small. It can be very easy to fall into a cycle of always wanting the next best thing rather than being content with the material possessions God has provided.

Please don't misunderstand! *Enjoying* God's blessings is not a sin; *coveting* things He has not given is. God will often bestow blessings upon His people that have never even entered into their hearts as desires or dreams! He delights in giving to His children, and we should view those gifts as blessings from Him. We must steward them for His glory, use them for His purposes, and be ever grateful for His daily provision in our lives. You don't need to feel guilty if God has blessed you with nice things—you should feel grateful.

Someone once said that contentment is "wanting what you have and not wanting what you don't have." This definition is basic, yet convicting! Simply make sure that, like the Apostle Paul, you are content with whatever God gives you and with any circumstance He allows to take place in your life.

Ministry Discontent

Sometimes we are discontent with our ministries. Are you discouraged because of the size or location of your church? Are you content being the nursery director because no one else wants the job? Are you joyful with where God has placed you in the ministry in general? Friend, God is sovereign, and He has placed you right where you are for a purpose. His desire for you is that you would be joyfully content right there until He sees fit to change your circumstances.

I read a story that illustrates what our outlook in life often becomes during times of discontentment. It goes like this:

> It was spring, but it was summer I wanted. I wanted the warm days and the great outdoors. It was summer, but it was fall I wanted—the colorful leaves and the cool, dry air. It was fall, but it was winter I wanted— the beautiful snow and the joy of the holiday season. It was winter, but it was spring I wanted—the warmth and blossoming of nature. I was a child, but it was adulthood I wanted—the freedom and respect. I was twenty, but it was thirty I wanted—to be more mature and sophisticated. I was middle-aged, but it was twenty I wanted—the youth and the free spirit. I was retired, but it was middle age I wanted—the presence of mind without limitations. Then my life was over, and I never got what I wanted.

We live in the desert, and so many times I wonder, "Will the heat of the summer ever end?" But by the time winter comes, I am ready for the warmth again. It reminds me of a little poem I heard. "As a rule, man's a fool. When it's hot, he wants it cool, and when it's cool, he wants it hot—always wanting what it's not." Often we find ourselves looking on the other side of the fence.

In *US News and World Report,* there was an article on the American dream. A poll was conducted which asked citizens, "How much money would you need to fulfill your American dream?" When they compiled the answers, they found that those who had an income of under $25,000 a year said it would take about $54,000 to fulfill their dream. Those people who had an income of $100,000 said it would take about $192,000 to fulfill their dream.[3]

We always think if we just had a little bit more, we would have everything we wanted. And, in the process, we become people who are never satisfied.

If we are not careful, we can look at other ministries and think, "Well, if we could only go to that church and serve, everything would be better." Friend, the solution to our discouragement is not another ministry or someone else's blessings. The solution is contentment! Paul said to Timothy in 1 Timothy 6:6, *"But godliness with contentment is great gain."* Again he admonished the Christians at Philippi, *"Not that I speak in respect of want: for I have learned, in whatsoever state I am, therewith to be content"* (Philippians 4:11).

My husband prays for and counsels with many pastors who tell him, "If we could just find another ministry where we can serve, that would make the positive difference in our situation." Often, these couples are experiencing problems or trials where they are serving. Rather than committing themselves to work through and grow through the trial, they are looking for greener pastures. They are looking for a place with no problems—a place that doesn't exist.

I am not trying to imply that it is never the will of God for people to relocate to another ministry. Surely, sometimes God does desire to move us, but we must be sure that we are following His leading and not our own feelings of discontentment.

Pride and discontentment—the two most common reasons pastors' wives become frustrated and discouraged in ministry. These sinful attitudes cause many women to ultimately forsake the will of God for their lives and destroy the ministries of their husbands in the process. Friend, don't underestimate the devil's desire to take you out of ministry and to use you to hurt or hinder what God desires to accomplish through your husband.

> *Not that I speak in respect of want: for I have learned, in whatsoever state I am, therewith to be content.*—PHILIPPIANS 4:11

CHAPTER FIVE

Nurturing Your Soul

*W*herefore do ye spend money for that which is not
bread? and your labour for that which satisfieth not?
hearken diligently unto me, and eat ye that which is
*good, and let your soul delight itself in fatness. Incline your ear, and
come unto me: hear, and your soul shall live; and I will make an
everlasting covenant with you, even the sure mercies of David.*
—Isaiah 55:2–3

One of the things we must do to stay alive is eat! Along with
air, water, and sleep, our bodies need *food*. The nutrients contained
in the food we eat keep us healthy and strong. If we neglect to
nourish our physical bodies, our health will inevitably decline.

The human soul works the same way! We must regularly
feed on God's Word to stay alive and spiritually healthy. We must
continually and purposefully nurture our souls with the Word of
God. First Peter 2:2 says, *"As newborn babes, desire the sincere milk*

of the word, that ye may grow thereby." And Job 23:12 says, *"Neither have I gone back from the commandment of his lips; I have esteemed the words of his mouth more than my necessary food."*

Spending time in Bible reading and prayer is to our spiritual lives what eating and resting is to our physical lives. Obviously, the less we eat and rest, the weaker we become. Even so, the less time you spend with the Lord, the weaker you will become against the attacks of Satan.

When we deprive ourselves of the nutrition found in the Bible, the "junk food" of this world becomes dangerously sweet to our spiritual senses. Proverbs 27:7 says, *"The full soul loatheth an honeycomb; but to the hungry soul every bitter thing is sweet."*

So, how is your spiritual appetite right now? Are you strong in the Lord? Are you hungry for quality time with God? Or, have you been feasting on the junk food of this world? Perhaps you are weak, in need of a structured diet to restore your spiritual health.

In the following pages, I'd like to share some ways to increase your spiritual appetite. I invite you to begin (or to continue) the satisfying process of nurturing your soul in the Word of God.

Our Appetite

When my children were babies, I took them to the doctor for periodical checkups. One of the first questions the doctor would ask was, "How is their appetite?" A loss of appetite was one indication that something was wrong. I always knew my sick children were feeling better when their appetites returned.

Some of us are starving spiritually, and we don't even realize it! God created us with a physical desire to eat several times a day, and He designed our spiritual lives with that same inner desire. Someone wisely said that the Bible is *everyday food*, not just medicine for emergencies! Yet, oftentimes, we reach for the Bible only when faced by a crisis or urgent need, and time with God is our last resort rather than our first impulse.

An appetite can come naturally or it can be acquired over time. When you became a Christian, the Holy Spirit took up residence in your life and gave birth to new appetites. So, if you don't have a spiritual hunger for the Bible, then one of two things may be wrong.

First, you may be spoiling your appetite with sin. It could be that your spiritual stomach is filled with other things.

When my children were little, they would occasionally come to the dinner table claiming that they weren't hungry. It never took us long to find evidence of the candy that had been eaten before dinner—and that candy never failed to rob their appetites. As Christians, if we don't have a hunger for Scripture, we too should investigate to see if we have unconfessed sin in our lives or if we are filling our lives with other "foods" that take away our desire for God's Word.

Second, you may not have acquired a taste for the Scriptures. Until a few years ago, I would never eat crème brulee. I just knew I would not like it. It didn't appeal to me at all! But there came a moment when my appetite changed forever!

We were having dinner with Dr. David Gibbs, and he ordered crème brulee for everyone at the table. Not wanting to offend him, I decided to go ahead and take at least one bite. I have been hooked from that moment on! Next to ice cream, crème brulee is now my favorite dessert. I have acquired a taste for it. Perhaps your appetite for God's Word is something that needs to be developed. May I encourage you to simply taste it? I guarantee that soon enough, you will be hooked!

As Christians, we tend to think that the Bible knowledge we gain from regular church attendance is enough to fill our appetites. This is a very unhealthy rationalization! Spending time in God's Word only at church would be like eating only a few pre-prepared meals a week. A spiritual diet consisting solely of what others have prepared for you is like exclusively eating canned food and TV dinners. God wants us to have some "good ol' home cooking"! He wants you to spend time personally preparing, tasting, and savoring His Word.

When you discover how truly good Bible study "tastes," you will find yourself going back for more.

> The longer you read the Bible, the more you will like it; it will grow sweeter and sweeter; and the more you get into the spirit of it, the more you will get into the spirit of Christ.—Romaine

Jeremiah 15:16 says, *"Thy words were found, and I did eat them; and thy word was unto me the joy and rejoicing of mine heart: for I am called by thy name, O LORD God of hosts."* And in Psalm 119:103 we are reminded, *"How sweet are thy words unto my taste! yea, sweeter than honey to my mouth!"* I challenge you to prove Psalm 34:8, *"O taste and see that the LORD is good: blessed is the man that trusteth in him."*

Advantages of Bible Study

I recently heard the following story that I believe best illustrates the importance of consistent Bible study:

> When their son left for his freshman year at Duke University, his parents gave him a Bible, assuring him it would be a great help. Later, as he began sending them letters asking for money, they would write back telling him to read his Bible, citing chapter and verse. He would reply that he was reading the Bible—but he still needed money. When he came home for a semester break, his parents told him they knew he had not been reading his Bible. How? They had tucked $10 and $20 bills by the verses they had cited in their letters.

It would have been very advantageous for that young man to have read his Bible!

Obviously, you probably won't find $20 bills when you read God's Word, but the benefits you will receive far exceed any monetary value! Here is just a short list of advantages to reading the Word of God:

- It is the way to grow spiritually—1 Peter 2:2; Matthew 4:4
- It is the way to grow in faith—Romans 10:17–18
- It is the way to have victory over sin—Psalm 119:9–12
- It is the "seed" for our witnessing—Luke 8:11; 1 Peter 1:23; Psalm 126:5–6
- It is how our heart stays tender—Jeremiah 23:29
- It is where we obtain God's wisdom—Psalm 19:7
- It is how the Lord guides us—Psalm 119:105
- It gives instruction in every doctrine—2 Timothy 3:16
- It is the way to have great peace—Psalm 119:165
- It is our strength—Psalm 119:28
- It is our assurance of salvation—1 John 5:13
- It is the way to know God's will—Psalm 119:104–105
- It gives us spiritual discernment—Psalm 119:130
- It is the way to be comforted—Psalm 119:52
- It is the way to experience answers to prayer—John 15:7
- It is our hope—Psalm 119:81
- It is the way to find joy—Psalm 119:111
- It leads to true success—Joshua 1:8
- It is the way to know God more intimately—John 1:1

What an encouraging list! There are so many blessings to claim as a result of consistent, meaningful time in God's Word. Don't settle for anything less!

The Adversary

The devil knows that he can defeat you if he can keep you away from the Word of God. If you have committed yourself to nurturing your spiritual appetite, you can be sure that you will face daily opposition. R. G. Lee said, "If you wake up in the morning and don't meet the devil face-to-face, it just might mean you're headed in the same direction!"

Our adversary, the devil, works to hinder us from partaking of our spiritual meals and to tempt us with unhealthy alternatives. There are a few areas in particular that I believe can become hindrances to our walk with God. Ask the Lord to help you be on guard as you resist the attacks of the enemy.

Wasting Time. The devil will use any device he can to accomplish his goal of spiritual weakness. In the day in which we live, the television is probably the worst enemy of Bible study. The average eighteen-year-old American has already watched 18,000 hours of TV. Experts tell us that by the time a TV-raised-American reaches the age of sixty-five, he will have had an average of 9½ years of solid TV viewing. That's fifteen percent of a person's life spent in front of a television set! On the other hand, if a person attended Sunday school regularly from birth until the age of sixty-five, he would only have had a total of four months of solid Bible teaching!

Perhaps TV isn't your weakness. But, most likely, there is an area in your life that can be identified as a "time waster." Determine to eliminate this hindrance to your walk with God!

Fatigue. The devil often uses another tactic to discourage us from spending time with God—he exaggerates our fatigue. We are somehow convinced that we are too tired to invest in our spiritual well-being. We face this battle when we wake up in the morning to have devotions! Henry Ward Beecher said, "The first hour of the morning is the rudder of the day." It's no wonder Satan fights so hard to keep us from spending this time with God! Here are some tips to help us win this battle:

- Go to bed on time.
- Get up as soon as the alarm goes off.
- Go to bed with the attitude of, "See you in the morning, Lord!" (The morning is not the time to pray about getting up! Pray for power and energy the night before!)

Ask God for the discipline to wake up and talk to Him each morning, and anticipate what He will do in your life as a result.

And in the morning, rising up a great while before day, he went out, and departed into a solitary place, and there prayed.
—MARK 1:35

Disinterest. Satan also works to make our devotions boring or disinteresting. Do you ever feel that you just don't seem to get much out of your quiet time? This is a lie! The Word of God is always working in you, whether you feel it or not.

I've had people tell me, "I don't remember what I read when I have my devotions, so it's obviously not making that much of a difference." Well, I don't remember what I ate for breakfast yesterday, but I know that I ate! And those nutrients sustained me throughout the day. A strainer doesn't hold any water, but at least it stays clean. Even so, if you feel that you are not retaining what you are reading, at least the Word of God is keeping your mind and heart clean on a daily basis.

Don't decide to have devotions based on how you feel. Emotions may lie, and feelings will come and go. If you have your devotions only when you feel like it, the devil will make sure you never feel like it. Have your time with the Lord because it is right and because you know your spiritual health is dependent upon it.

It is true that there may be long periods of "dryness" in your devotional life. But, please don't become discouraged or disinterested in your relationship with the Lord during these times. Instead, ask God to show you what may be causing the lack of excitement. Perhaps you struggle with one of the following:

- ◆ Disobedience: Resolve unconfessed sin in your life.
- ◆ Physical fatigue: Be sure you are well rested when you spend time with God.
- ◆ Urgency: Don't be in a hurry. Remember it takes time to develop a relationship with the Lord (just as it does with people). Read until you find the truth He wants to communicate to you.

- Independence: Have you been living apart from God for too long? Humbly return, and ask Him to renew your dependence on Him.

Distractions. If you have won these first few battles, the devil will probably attack you by sending some distractions along the way. Have you ever noticed how many "to do's" come to mind while you're having devotions? The devil will try to get your mind to wander in all directions during your quiet time. Here are some suggestions to help avoid this tactic:

- Purpose to be alert: Splash water on your face, open a window, walk, or move around.
- Read and pray aloud: Don't be embarrassed to do this! It will greatly help your mind stay attentive to the Lord.
- Jot thoughts down: Keep a notebook handy to write down those "things" you can't forget, so that your mind can continue to focus on God!

Lack of Discipline. Perhaps the greatest struggle for maintaining a consistent quiet time is the ability to *faithfully* "stick to it." So, here are some tips to help you discipline yourself to cultivate your relationship with God consistently:

- Make a vow to God. Commit yourself and your time to Him. Schedule a specific time to meet with God daily.
- Expect and be prepared for the devil's distractions and attacks.
- Leave your Bible open the night before to the passage you intend to read in the morning.
- Never allow an exception to occur until the new habit is securely rooted in your life. (Allow thirty days to form a new habit.)
- Rely on God's power. Remember this is a spiritual battle.

Ask God

I need the Lord's help in every area of my life—including my quiet time with Him! I ask for His help as I strive to grow closer to Him. First, I ask Him to help me remain faithful. Second, I pray for an understanding of what I am reading. Third, I ask the Lord to show me something about Him from the Scripture that I can apply to my life that day.

Author Nancy Leigh DeMoss gives this advice for preparing your heart in prayer: "Ask God to quiet your heart and to speak to you through His Word. Ask Him to shine the light of His truth into your life. In this quiet moment, surrender yourself to Him and commit to obey whatever He shows you."

Begin your time of devotions by praying these Scriptures:

Open thou mine eyes, that I may behold wondrous things out of thy law.—PSALM 119:18

Give me understanding, and I shall keep thy law; yea, I shall observe it with my whole heart.—PSALM 119:34

Shew me thy ways, O LORD; teach me thy paths. Lead me in thy truth, and teach me: for thou art the God of my salvation; on thee do I wait all the day.—PSALM 25:4–5

That which I see not teach thou me: if I have done iniquity, I will do no more.—JOB 34:32

The Appointment

Nurturing your soul is not something that will happen by chance—it must be deliberate. You must take time to cultivate your walk with God.

If you have not already done so, make a commitment to the Lord that you will spend time with Him every day. Set an appointment with God just as you would a doctor's appointment or another appointment on your daily agenda. Establish a time and a place, and do not cancel it!

If it is at all feasible, make this appointment the first one of your day. There have been mornings when I was running behind and decided to have my devotions later. When "later" finally came and I read the Word of God, I was amazed at how those verses would have helped me earlier in the day.

Most health experts agree on one thing—always eat breakfast! We need our *spiritual* breakfast! If mornings truly aren't the best time for you, then schedule your appointment for later in the day when you feel you can be most attentive. But, as you strive to nurture your soul, I encourage you to meditate on *at least* one verse or passage of Scripture before entering into the busyness of your day. It will provide the needed strength and encouragement to get you through your daily schedule.

Just as a runner would stretch to prepare his muscles for the endurance of the race, so we must "warm-up" our spiritual muscle, the heart, to prepare for our daily marathon!

After you have assigned a time, establish a place where you can be alone with God. Jesus had a set place to where He resorted when He was on this earth. When Judas betrayed Jesus, he knew exactly where He would be. John 18:2 says, *"And Judas also, which betrayed him, knew the place: for Jesus ofttimes resorted thither with his disciples."*

We learn from Daniel's life that he was found guilty of praying in his chamber three times a day as he always did. Daniel 6:10 says, *"Now when Daniel knew that the writing was signed, he went into his house; and his windows being open in his chamber toward Jerusalem, he kneeled upon his knees three times a day, and prayed, and gave thanks before his God, as he did aforetime."* Jesus and Daniel, as well as others in the Bible, had an established place to spend time with God.

In a letter to his friends, hymn writer Wendell P. Loveless related this story:

> One evening a speaker who was visiting the United States wanted to make a telephone call. He entered a phone booth, but found it to be different from those in his own country. It was beginning to get dark, so

he had difficulty finding the number in the directory. He noticed that there was a light in the ceiling, but he didn't know how to turn it on. As he tried again to find the number in the fading twilight, a passerby noted his plight and said, "Sir, if you want to turn the light on, you have to shut the door." To the visitor's amazement and satisfaction, when he closed the door, the booth was filled with light. He soon located the number and completed the call.

In a similar way, when we draw aside to a quiet place to pray, we must block out our busy world and open our hearts to the Father. Our darkened world of disappointments and trials will then be illuminated. We will enter into communion with God; we will sense His presence, and we will be assured of His provision for us.

Attempt a Different Approach

It is imperative to our spiritual survival that we are *daily* in the Word of God. Spurgeon said, "We quickly lose the nourishment and strength of yesterday's bread. We must feed our souls daily upon the manna God has given us." First Timothy 4:13 says, *"Till I come, give attendance to reading…."* Because reading God's Word is a command, we must consistently stick to a plan. Our approach cannot be hit and miss.

When I eat at a familiar restaurant, I enjoy trying something new every now and then. I like variety! When I have my time with God, I like to incorporate variety in my approach as well.

It could be easy to fall into a routine during our quiet time with the Lord. Yet, there are different ways to read God's Word, and I encourage you to vary your approach from time to time to keep your devotions fresh and vibrant. Here are a few methods to consider incorporating into your devotional life.

Read God's Word. Vary your approach to reading God's Word. You may want to read the books of the Bible in chronological order, or pick a particular book of the Bible to read through several times. There are many different Bible-reading schedules you can follow.

- Read through the Bible in a year.
- Read one Proverb a day, corresponding with the day of the month.
- Read through the book of Psalms in one month (Read five chapters a day by dividing the chapters accordingly: The day of the month plus 30, plus 60, plus 90, plus 120. For example, on January 1, you would read Psalm 1, 31, 61, 91, and 121.)
- Read fifteen minutes per day.
- Read until you receive a blessing or a truth.

Study God's Word. Charles Spurgeon said, "Do not be content to just read the words of Scripture. Seek to grasp the message they contain." In addition to reading, we should *study* the Scriptures. Second Timothy 2:15 exhorts, *"Study to shew thyself approved unto God, a workman that needeth not to be ashamed, rightly dividing the word of truth."* Determine to intentionally read God's Word to understand the truths contained therein.

There are many ways to study the Bible. Consider doing a word or topical study—defining, memorizing, and applying a particular word or phrase. You may want to focus on different Bible characters or spend time exploring the attributes of God. Decide on a topic for study and journal what God teaches you.

Meditate on the Word of God. *Meditate* means "to ponder or to reflect." God commands us in Joshua 1:8 to meditate on His Word continually. *"This book of the law shall not depart out of thy mouth; but thou shalt meditate therein day and night, that thou mayest observe to do according to all that is written therein: for then thou shalt make thy way prosperous, and then thou shalt have good success."* It's easy to justify our lack of meditation: "I can't meditate *day and night*! How do you think about things that long?" May I say that if you can worry, you can meditate! I've never heard someone say that they have a hard time worrying! If you can mull over problems and personal situations with which you are dealing, you can mull over the promises of God!

Someone said, "Reading the Bible without meditating on it is like trying to eat without swallowing. Meditating on God's Word has been likened unto a cow digesting his food. The cow will bring up previously digested food for renewed chewing and preparation for absorption. As a Christian we should 'chew' on what we have read and absorb what we have read. The result will be enormous."

George Mueller's testimony challenges me on my meditation of Scripture: "The first evening that I shut myself into my room, to give myself to prayer and meditation over the Scriptures, I learned more in a few hours than I had done during a period of several months previously." When was the last time you "shut yourself into a room" for the sole purpose of meditating on the words and promises of God to you?

I try to remember three key words when meditating on God's Word.

- Visualize—Put yourself in the situation of the story which you are reading. When did this take place? How would I have felt? What circumstances led to this point?
- Emphasize—Read the verse, emphasizing each word or phrase. For example, read the following verse emphasizing the italicized word.

  "*I* can do all things through Christ which strengtheneth me."
  "I *can* do all things through Christ which strengtheneth me."
  "I can *do* all things through Christ which strengtheneth me."
  "I can do *all* things through Christ which strengtheneth me."
  "I can do all *things* through Christ which strengtheneth me."
  "I can do all things *through* Christ which strengtheneth me."
  "I can do all things through *Christ* which strengtheneth me."
  "I can do all things through Christ *which* strengtheneth me."
  "I can do all things through Christ which *strengtheneth* me."
  "I can do all things through Christ which strengtheneth *me*."

- Personalize—Put your name in the verse, as if it were written just for you. It was!

> *For God so loved* Terrie Chappell, *that he gave his only begotten Son, that* Terrie who *believeth in him should not perish, but have everlasting life.*—JOHN 3:16

Memorize the Word of God. We memorize our phone number, social security number, bank account number, our driver's license number, numerous passwords and pin numbers; but how many Bible verses have we committed to memory? Bible memory is a discipline, and unfortunately, it is not practiced enough among Christians.

Bible memory allows us to take God's Word with us wherever we go. You may be surprised when verses that have been committed to memory will come to your mind to keep you from sin or to give wisdom for the moment. Psalm 119:11 says, *"Thy word have I hid in mine heart, that I might not sin against thee."*

The Holy Spirit will cause you to remember verses as you witness, to give you hope, to help you flee temptation and to provide direction. Here are some ideas to help you memorize Scripture:

- Develop and follow a Bible memorization plan. How many verses do you want to memorize this week? What time has been set aside for Bible memory? What topics should I focus on? Is there an entire passage I should commit to memory?
- Read the verse and reference several times. Repetition is the key to learning! Read (and even write) the verses you are trying to memorize.
- Use the verse whenever you can. Look for situations in which to apply the verse you are committing to memory. Share it with others.
- Find someone to whom you can be accountable.

Write the Word of God. I am currently using this method of writing Scripture in my own personal devotions. I read the verse, say the verse, write the verse while saying the verse, and then say the verse from what I have written. My favorite benefit of using this method is that it will not let me skip or skim over even one word of Scripture. I must meditate on each and every one—not to mention it has given me a deeper appreciation for those early scribes!

Application

Application is the goal of our devotional time. Ask yourself, "How can what I read make me more like Christ?" "How can I apply this truth to my life today?" Francis Bacon wisely stated, "It is not what men eat but what they digest that makes them strong; not what we gain but what we save that makes us rich; not what we read but what we remember that makes us learned; not what we preach but what we practice that makes us Christians." The Bible is powerful and practical, but it must be applied to and lived out in our daily lives.

A.W. Tozer said, "Unused truth becomes as useless as an unused muscle." God desires that we put the truths we've learned into practice through obedience to His Word. When we refuse to obey the Scriptures, we are only hurting and deceiving ourselves.

> *But be ye doers of the word, and not hearers only, deceiving your own selves.*—JAMES 1:22

God also wants an immediate response to His Word. We teach our children that delayed obedience is disobedience. So, decide that you will obey your Heavenly Father right away!

> *I thought on my ways, and turned my feet unto thy testimonies. I made haste, and delayed not to keep thy commandments.*
> —PSALM 119:59–60

The following four statements provide helpful criteria when seeking to apply Scripture to our hearts and lives:

- ◆   Our applications should be personal.
- ◆   Our applications should be practical.
- ◆   Our applications should be possible.
- ◆   Our applications should be provable.

One night an admiral on a u.s. Navy battleship ordered a certain course. The navigation officer, seeing a light in the distance, reported that the battleship now seemed to be on a collision course with another ship. So the admiral ordered his radio officer to send a message to the oncoming ship that it should change its course ten degrees to the south. The reply came simply, "No. You change YOUR course ten degrees to the north." After two more unsuccessful exchanges, the admiral, now quite furious, came thundering into the radio control room, grabbed the microphone, and bellowed into it, "Do you know that you are talking to an ADMIRAL in the UNITED STATES NAVY!" After a brief moment of silence, the even-tempered reply came back, "Sir, do you know that YOU are talking to the lighthouse?"

When God asks you to change your course, remember Who you are talking to and be willing to do whatever He asks!

Adjust our Attitude

There is a story of a young English pianist who gave his inaugural concert to a full house in a London hall. His music was brilliant, and when he finished, the crowd gave him a long standing ovation. Young and shy, he retreated backstage. The stage manager urged him to return for a bow and an encore, but the young pianist refused. "The entire audience is standing and clapping for you," the manager said, insisting that the pianist return to the stage. "Not everyone is standing," the young musician replied. "There is a gray-haired man in the balcony who remains seated." The manager peeked out. "You're right," he said. "But everyone else is standing. He makes no difference. Don't worry about him. Just go back there." The young pianist replied, "He is my teacher and unless he stands, I haven't met the standards."

That young pianist was motivated by the approval of his teacher. Jesus is our Teacher, and unless He is pleased with the attitude and spirit in which we approach Him, we are failing in our relationship with Him. God reminded Samuel that the Lord does not see as man sees. Man looks at the outward appearance, but the Lord focuses on the heart.

In God's eyes, *why* we do something is far more important than *what* we do. Why do you spend time with God? Is it out of a sense of duty or out of a heart of love for Him? How is your attitude as you enter God's presence? Is it one of heartless service or humble surrender?

It is quite possible to do the right thing but with the wrong attitude. This was Amaziah's problem. Second Chronicles 25:2 records, *"And he did that which was right in the sight of the LORD, but not with a perfect heart."* So, what characteristics should our heart toward God possess?

First, we must have a pure heart. Jesus said, *"Blessed are the pure in heart"* (Matthew 5:8). Make sure your sins are confessed, and that there is nothing between you and the Saviour.

Second, come before the Lord with an attitude of reverence. Life is very busy, so be careful to not rush into God's presence. Be still, and let the quietness clear away the cares of the world. Habakkuk 2:20 says, *"But the LORD is in his holy temple: let all the earth keep silence before him."*

Third, be alert and pay attention. Remember you are meeting with the God of the universe, your Creator—your Saviour. He deserves an acute awareness of His presence and complete attention to His Word.

Fourth, have a heart of complete surrender. This attitude is so important. Don't pick and choose what you will obey. Come before the Lord having already chosen to do His will—no matter what!

Last, we should have a spirit of expectancy. Let's come before God with anticipation and eagerness. Expect to have a good time with your God and to receive a blessing from Him.

A circuit-riding preacher entered a church building with his young son and dropped a coin into the offering box in the back.

Not many came that Sunday, and those who did weren't very excited about what was said. After the service, the preacher and son walked to the back, and he emptied the box. Only the one coin fell out. The young boy said, "Dad, if you'd have put more in, you'd have gotten more out!"

The more that we invest in our study of the Bible, the more we will get out of it! How much time and effort have you put into your devotional time? Are you allowing time for God's Word to shape your mind and change your thinking?

Adjust your attitude to one of expectancy. Believe that God will reveal Himself and His truths to you personally!

Accountability

The story is told of early African converts to Christianity who were sincere and consistent in their private devotions. Each one reportedly had a separate spot in a thicket where he would pour out his heart to God. Over time, the paths to these places became well worn. As a result, if one of these believers began to neglect his prayer time, it was soon apparent to the others. They would kindly remind the negligent one, "Brother, the grass grows on your path."

Have you given someone in your life the liberty to say, "The grass is growing on your path"? Let me encourage you to be accountable in your walk with God. Ask a spouse or a friend to hold you accountable in your devotions. Allow this person to ask questions, wake you up in the morning, listen to memorized verses, or do whatever it takes to encourage you in building a relationship with God.

> This Book is the mind of God, the state of man, the way of salvation, the doom of sinners, and the happiness of believers. Its doctrines are holy, its precepts are binding; its histories are true, and its decisions are immutable. Read it to be wise, believe

it to be safe, practice it to be holy. It contains light to direct you, food to support you, and comfort to cheer you. It is the traveler's map, the pilgrim's staff, the pilot's compass, the soldier's sword, and the Christian's character. Here paradise is restored, Heaven opened, and the gates of hell disclosed. Christ is its grand subject, our good its design, and the glory of God its end. It should fill the memory, rule the heart, and guide the feet. Read it slowly, frequently, prayerfully. It is a mine of wealth, a paradise of glory, and a river of pleasure. Follow its precepts and it will lead you to Calvary, to the empty tomb, to a resurrected life in Christ; yes, to glory itself, for eternity.

—Author Unknown

CHAPTER SIX

Overcoming Personal Obstacles

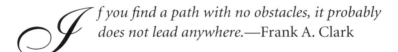

I f you find a path with no obstacles, it probably does not lead anywhere.—Frank A. Clark

Identifying Your Obstacles

During my last four semesters of high school P.E., I finally discovered a sport that I really enjoyed playing—tennis! I played tennis every chance I had, and considering that I'm not the athletic type, I did pretty well. I knew the rules, I had the fundamentals down, and I actually won quite a few matches.

In spite of this, there was one person who consistently defeated me. My biggest rival on the court, though, was not the person across the net—it was me! It seemed when I needed a point the most, I would make an error. I would double fault, my shot would go long, or worse yet, I would miss the ball completely! *I* was my biggest obstacle.

Early in my marriage, I found that the same was true in my life and ministry. I was my own worst enemy. The biggest obstacle I had to overcome was myself. I was insecure about becoming a pastor's wife. In my mind, I had a list of reasons why God could not use me. My reasoning constantly reminded me: *I am too shy, I wasn't raised in a Christian home, I don't know what to say*—and the list goes on. I just didn't think I could fit the mold of a pastor's wife. These feelings of inadequacy were huge personal obstacles that I had to overcome.

There is a tale of a lady having surgery. While on the operating table, something went wrong and she died. As she was entering Heaven, Peter told her that there had been a mistake. It wasn't her time to die. The lady asked Peter if this was a joke or if she would really continue to live. Peter confirmed that she would indeed live to be an old lady.

So the doctors brought her back to life, and as soon as she was released from the hospital, she made an appointment with a plastic surgeon. She had a face-lift and a tummy tuck. Then she colored her hair and had her nails done.

As soon as she left the nail salon, she stepped off the curb and walked directly in front of an oncoming car. The car hit her and she died again. She was a little upset to meet Peter the second time—having spent all that time and money to have a makeover. She said to Peter, "I thought I had another forty years."

Peter replied, "Oh, I'm sorry, I didn't recognize you!"

And the moral of the story is—be yourself!

*I will praise thee; for I am fearfully and wonderfully made: marvellous are thy works; and that my soul knoweth right well. My substance was not hid from thee, when I was made in secret, and curiously wrought in the lowest parts of the earth. Thine eyes did see my substance, yet being unperfect; and in thy book all my members were written, which in continuance were fashioned, when as yet there was none of them. How precious also are thy thoughts unto me, O God! how great is the sum of them!—*Psalm 139:14–17

God wants us to accept ourselves just the way He created us to be, recognizing we are His precious, one-of-a-kind treasure. It seems that women (like the one we just read about) spend a lot of time, money, and energy attempting to "get another look" or update their style in an effort to cover or eliminate their feelings of insecurity and inadequacy. They are not content with who they are in Christ.

Because Prince William and Prince Harry of England were born into the royal family, they have received a certain type of status and worth. We would call this "assigned worth." Those boys have done nothing to deserve their position in society; it is simply a part of their birthright. As Christians, we also have assigned worth! We are children of the King, and God says we are valuable in His sight! We don't deserve our position of "royal standing" before the Lord, but we have it because of our birth in Christ.

Ephesians 1:3–9 gives this promise: *"Blessed be the God and Father of our Lord Jesus Christ, who hath blessed us with all spiritual blessings in heavenly places in Christ: According as he hath chosen us in him before the foundation of the world, that we should be holy and without blame before him in love: Having predestinated us unto the adoption of children by Jesus Christ to himself, according to the good pleasure of his will, To the praise of the glory of his grace, wherein he hath made us accepted in the beloved. In whom we have redemption through his blood, the forgiveness of sins, according to the riches of his grace; Wherein he hath abounded toward us in all wisdom and prudence; Having made known unto us the mystery of his will, according to his good pleasure which he hath purposed in himself."*

Think about the phrase, "accepted in the beloved." So often, we look to everyone but our Heavenly Father for acceptance and affirmation. God is the One who loves us in spite of our fears and frustrations! We don't have to "fake it" around Him. He wants to use the weaknesses of our lives to draw us closer to Him.

You may feel invaluable, worn, tired, or useless in the work of the ministry. But this does not mean that you have lost your value in the Lord's work! A twenty-dollar bill is worth twenty dollars whether it is new and crisp or tattered, wrinkled, and old. Even so, we as God's children never lose our assigned worth in Christ! We are accepted in the beloved!

The American Heritage Dictionary defines *acceptance* as "to receive gladly; take willingly; and a belief in something." Let's use this definition to observe the factors that trigger insecurities in the heart of a Christian servant.

Our Past: "To Receive Gladly"

First, let's look at the insecurity of our past. Most of us have an area in our house where we store our keepsakes, holiday decorations, and other infrequently used items. At our house, that area is over the garage in the attic. In a similar way, we all have an internal "attic" in our lives where our past is stored: past ministry failures, past family heartaches, past personal trials. In this internal attic, we keep our memories, our failures, our disappointments, and our hurts. The sad truth is that our past can come back to haunt us to the point that it makes us feel completely inadequate, unacceptable, and discouraged in the Lord's work.

The Apostle Paul had a terrible background that could have constantly haunted and limited him in the ministry. He says in Philippians 3:13, *"Brethren, I count not myself to have apprehended: but this one thing I do, forgetting those things which are behind, and reaching forth unto those things which are before."*

We all have things in our past that we regret, but we don't have to let these things control us. Someone once said, "The person whose problems are all behind him is probably a school bus driver." We cannot change past circumstances, but we *can* lessen their influence and control on our lives today.

The story is told of two men talking, and one man said, "Every time my wife and I have an argument she becomes historical." The other man said, "Don't you mean hysterical?" The first man replied, "No, I mean historical. She starts bringing up the past!" Forgetting is hard, isn't it? Satan constantly reminds us of our past and tries to intimidate us from serving God. I like what one preacher said, "When Satan brings up your past, remind him of his future!" Do not let your past influence today! Remember, forgetting is not a memory *lapse*, it is a memory *release*.

Several years ago, we had a Mother-Daughter-Friend Tea with the theme, "If Friends Were Flowers, I'd Pick You." As you could imagine with that title, we incorporated a lot of clay pots! It seemed we had hundreds of clay pots at that event. We decorated them, used them as centerpieces, and even served food in them!

In all of the activity of preparation, some of these pots were broken. Since we couldn't find any more pots around town, we decided to use the cracked pots as candle-holders. To our delight we discovered that broken pots made better candle-holders than the new pots because the cracks allowed the candlelight to shine through. May I remind you, in case you've forgotten recently; *we're* made of clay! Your clay vessel may have cracks and flaws, but like those clay pots, the light of Christ can shine through you in such a way that even your "cracks" are used to the glory of God. You can become a trophy of God's grace.

> But he giveth more grace. Wherefore he saith, God resisteth the proud, but giveth grace unto the humble.—JAMES 4:6

> That the name of our Lord Jesus Christ may be glorified in you, and ye in him, according to the grace of our God and the Lord Jesus Christ.—2 THESSALONIANS 1:12

> And he said unto me, My grace is sufficient for thee: for my strength is made perfect in weakness. Most gladly therefore will I

rather glory in my infirmities, that the power of Christ may rest upon me.—2 Corinthians 12:9

I once heard a story about another kind of vessel. This vessel was a beautiful vase, and it sat very nicely in a spacious living room. The lady of the house told her two sons not to play in that room because she didn't want her beautiful vase broken. One day the mother left the two boys home while she ran an errand, and while she was gone, the two boys began to play ball in the living room. Sure enough, a few moments later, they broke the vase.

Hurriedly the two boys began to glue it back together and a few moments later, it was impossible to tell that the vase had even been broken. Several months went by and the mother never even noticed that the vase had been broken.

One day as she was dusting the living room, she accidentally knocked the vase over, and it broke again. She too began to glue it back together and noticed that it had been broken once before. The strange thing was that it didn't break where it had previously been glued. The vessel was actually stronger in those places.

I thank God that when He restores our lives, we can actually be stronger because of His healing grace! Let's not hold onto a broken past and become bitter. Choose to accept it gladly, trusting that God has a purpose for every situation in our lives! Let the Lord put us together again and make us stronger because of what has happened in our past.

The Bible is filled with examples of how God delights in taking various backgrounds and using them for His glory. Joseph had brothers who were very cruel and sold him into slavery. Rahab lived the life of a harlot. Mary Magdalene was possessed with seven devils. Paul murdered Christians. Ruth lost her husband. Timothy was fatherless. This is just a short list, but God used these people in spite of their backgrounds. Joseph ruled under Pharaoh, preparing for the seven-year famine. Rahab showed faith and helped two of God's spies escape. Mary

Magdalene was at the tomb of Jesus. Paul became a mighty missionary for Christ. Ruth followed Naomi into a foreign land and there married Boaz. Timothy became a wonderful pastor.

Friend, God has given to each of us a different past, and He intends to use those differences for His glory in the present. Someone once said, "Never cling to the past so tightly that it leaves your arms unable to embrace the present." Your past—accept it gladly!

Our Present: "To Take Willingly"

Not only can our past affect our ability to serve the Lord effectively, but our present can as well. The devil desires to use present circumstances to hinder us from glorifying God the way we should.

Limited by the Physical

First, take a look at your physical limitations. Is there something about your physical appearance that hinders your spirit and robs your joy? Have you thought, "I'm too fat, I'm too short, I'm not pretty, I'm not in style, I'm…"? These kinds of statements will thwart your service to the Lord. Paul testified that he experienced physical limitations in ministry: "*And lest I should be exalted above measure through the abundance of the revelations, there was given to me a thorn in the flesh, the messenger of Satan to buffet me, lest I should be exalted above measure*" (2 Corinthians 12:7). He chose not to allow his "thorn in the flesh" to hinder his service to the Lord. Ask God to help you *willingly* accept any physical limitations you may be unhappy with in your life.

Helen Keller, who was blind and deaf, said, "So much has been given to me, I have no time to ponder over that which has been denied." She realized that she had been fashioned in God's image and that she had been blessed with worth and acceptance—blessings of eternal, rather than physical, value. May we have that spirit of gratitude for what God has given to us!

Hindered by Personality

Second, let's consider our personality traits and personal abilities. For some people, personality and abilities are legitimate obstacles to overcome. We tend to blame our personality for *not* doing what we *should* be doing or for *doing* what we should *not* be doing! For example, I am a shy person by nature. Growing up, when the doorbell rang, I would hide. I didn't want to be seen. In school, I would have rather taken a failing grade than stand before the class for an oral report or speech. My mom never had to tell me not to talk to strangers—I didn't talk to *anyone*.

Even now as an adult, I am still a shy person deep inside. I would be content to stay home and read a book and never talk to anyone. It would be easy for me not to greet visitors at church, never to share the plan of salvation with anyone, or not to be involved in ministry because I'm shy. I could easily justify these things because of my personality. Yet God does not want me to use my shyness as an excuse not to serve Him. He wants to take my weaknesses and make them strong by His grace.

Maybe you have other excuses like: "I'm just not a people person," "I'm a private person," "I just have a loud voice," "I can't help that I am critical and easily irritated, that's the way God made me." Review this list, and ask the Lord to reveal any areas of needed improvement in your life:

- Compulsive talking
- Habitual lateness
- Critical spirit
- Pettiness (seeing molehills as mountains)
- Lack of emotional control
- Strong individualism which stifles teamwork
- Passivity—overly reserved
- Over-commitment to too many things
- Laziness
- Poor time management and priorities

Beware of rationalizing bad behavior by saying, "That's just *naturally* how I am." Naturally, we are all sinners. When we trusted Christ, God gave us new natures. He gave us the ability by the power of His Spirit to change the way we "naturally are"! As Christians, it should be our desire to cultivate this new nature rather than just accepting the old one!

As we yield to God's Spirit, we will never use our personality or lack of ability as an excuse not to obey God or serve Him. Moses tried to make excuses. Look what he says in Exodus 4:10–12, *"And Moses said unto the LORD, O my Lord, I am not eloquent, neither heretofore, nor since thou hast spoken unto thy servant: but I am slow of speech, and of a slow tongue. And the LORD said unto him, Who hath made man's mouth? or who maketh the dumb, or deaf, or the seeing, or the blind? have not I the LORD? Now therefore go, and I will be with thy mouth, and teach thee what thou shalt say."*

Moses' excuses didn't hold up with God! God used him in a great way in spite of his weaknesses! God will take your inadequacies and use you to further His purpose as well!

Your personality may be on the other end of the spectrum. Perhaps you have a more outgoing temperament or possess great talent, and maybe you don't feel inadequate for the ministry at all!

If you are not careful, pride will keep you from experiencing the true blessings of how God intends to use you. Pride causes our natural ability to get in the way of Spirit-filled service. If you struggle in this area, decide to work at not limiting yourself to one strength or talent. For example, if you have a beautiful voice, give it to the Lord and use it for His glory. But don't develop an attitude that says, "I only sing solos!" Be a team player, and sing in the choir. When you are not singing, help in Sunday school or in the nursery. Be available and yielded to do *whatever* God wants you to do. Remember that your talents and abilities are gifts from God, so be a completely yielded vessel in the service of the Lord.

Intimidated by Perfectionism

Third, let's look at the obstacle of perfectionism. Frankly, *perfectionism* does not exist! The perfect child doesn't exist, nor does the perfect parent. There is no such thing as a perfect pastor, a perfect pastor's wife, or a perfect church member! Perfection is intangible in most situations because it is immeasurable.

When we are dealing with personal insecurity or when the devil is intimidating us with our past or present failures, we will tend to see others as "perfect." This perception begins an ungodly process of comparing ourselves to other people. The Scripture warns in 2 Corinthians 10:12, *"For we dare not make ourselves of the number, or compare ourselves with some that commend themselves: but they measuring themselves by themselves, and comparing themselves among themselves, are not wise."* Perfection will only be attained when we get to Heaven, so until then, we should strive to be like *Christ* in everything we do!

If you're struggling with any of these personal obstacles of the present—your physical limitations, personality, or lack of perfection—lay them at the feet of Jesus. Willingly embrace the obstacles of the present as opportunities of growth in your walk with the Lord.

Our Potential: "Belief in Something"

The third aspect in the American Heritage Dictionary definition of acceptance is to believe in something. Have you ever doubted whether or not God could really use you? Do you question your true potential for God? If you have attempted to serve the Lord at all, then you've probably dealt with this struggle of doubt—a lack of faith in God to accomplish His will in your life.

In His Word, God promises a place of usefulness and blessing to each of us. Jeremiah 29:11 says, *"For I know the thoughts that I think toward you, saith the LORD, thoughts of peace, and not of evil, to give you an expected end."*

There was a Peanuts comic in which Snoopy said, "Yesterday, I was a dog. Today, I am a dog. Tomorrow, I will probably be a dog. Sigh. There's so little hope for advancement." I think we can easily have Snoopy's same fatalistic approach to life, "This is just how I am and how things are going to be. There's so little hope for the future." If your hope is in God (and it should be), there is a wonderful promise for the future! God accepts you! He believes that with His help and empowerment, you can experience a future of service to Him that far exceeds your own expectations! God promises in 1 Corinthians 2:9, *"But as it is written, Eye hath not seen, nor ear heard, neither have entered into the heart of man, the things which God hath prepared for them that love him."* Simply learn to love and follow God, and choose to trust Him with your future.

The devil so deceitfully causes us to doubt our usefulness and purpose in God's plan. But no matter what you are facing today, there is hope. We *can* overcome obstacles of the past and present, and we can reach our potential to glorify God in the future!

Overcoming Your Obstacles

One of the greatest sources of encouragement to me over the years has been the simple truth, that with God, there is always potential for change! If you desire a true heart change for your future, then claim Luke 1:37, *"For with God nothing shall be impossible."* The famous Chinese proverbs says, "A journey of a thousand miles begins with a single step." The first step for us to overcome any obstacle is to ask God for help.

Be willing to be patient for change. The question is—are we willing to patiently allow change to occur on God's timetable? Usually we expect change to take place overnight, but lasting change always takes time.

I will lift up mine eyes unto the hills, from whence cometh my help. My help cometh from the LORD, which made heaven and earth.—PSALM 121:1–2

Measure our worth accurately by the Bible—not by our own comparisons. God's Word is filled with truth about who you are in Christ. I encourage you to memorize Scripture and claim verses when you feel worthless in life or ministry. Acknowledge God's truth of who you are in His sight, and rejoice in the fact that He fully accepts you and believes in your potential to accomplish His purposes!

Accept God's plan. Accepting God's plan involves letting go of your own and trusting Him for everything else.

If you are confident in your abilities and personality, then perhaps you need to learn to accept *God's* ways rather than your own. He may not want to accomplish His will the same way you do, so you must be sensitive to His leading and surrendered to His plan.

If you are only confident of your *limitations*, then learn to accept God's plan, as well! God did not make a mistake when He determined your life's destiny. He knew your infirmities and insecurities, and He still chose you to do His will.

A big part of the victory in overcoming personal obstacles is just surrendering to God's plan. Accept His purpose, embrace His call, and determine to obey even though it may not make sense.

A man was hiking high up in the mountains when he slipped and tumbled to a ledge below. Clinging for dear life he began to cry, "Hey, is anyone up there?" As his voice echoed off the canyon walls around him, he heard a strong, low reply, "Yes." "Who is it?" he shouted back. "It is God," replied the voice. "What do you want me to do?" asked the hiker. "Let go," said God. After a few awkward seconds of silence the hiker shouted, "Is anyone *else* up there?"

Accepting God's plan requires genuine faith on our part, and that faith will be expressed as you accept God's plan in spite of your own personal obstacles and limitations.

> A bird from his perch by the side of the sea
> Watched the fish jump and swim,
> And thought, "Fish are all free.
> To the floor of the ocean,

They can swim shore to shore
I want to be free—not a bird anymore."
But the fish watched the bird
And thought, "It's just not fair!
How I wish I were free! How I wish I could fly!
Such a sad state of bondage plagues
Fish such as I!"
So the fish jumped right out
And the bird dove right in
Seeking to find satisfaction within
But the fish couldn't fly and he died on the shore
And the bird couldn't swim
He was heard from no more.
When God created me, He had a purpose in mind
And a happier life's lot I never could find;
I am what He made me, because of His grace,
Right where God put me is life's happiest place.
I once sought to find greener grass somewhere else
And to be what God did not intend for myself,
But now I have learned I can only be free
If I accept and enjoy what He made me to be.

Apply God's Word. The Christian world is suffering from a deficiency in vitamin A—application! The last step to truly discovering our usefulness to God is to apply God's Word to our lives.

Application implies action! We need to commit to *doing* what is right no matter how it feels. I heard the following riddle recently: "If there were five frogs on a log and three of them decide to jump, how many frogs are left on the log?" The answer is *five*! There are still five frogs on the log because there is a difference between deciding to jump and actually jumping!

If you are to overcome the obstacles we've talked about in this chapter, you must commit to taking action. May I encourage you to make the following commitments:

- ♦   I will be patient with myself. God has entrusted me with the potential gifts, talents, and personality to do His perfect will. Philippians 2:13 says, *"For it is God which worketh in you both to will and to do of his good pleasure."*
- ♦   I will begin to improve the changeable areas as God directs. I will be sensitive and obedient to the leading of the Holy Spirit.
- ♦   I will seek to fulfill my potential by setting goals for myself.
- ♦   I will stop using my past or lack of abilities as an excuse.
- ♦   I will daily confess and forsake sin in my life.
- ♦   I will accept God's estimation of me—remembering He loved me enough to send His Son to die for me.
- ♦   I will endeavor to fulfill the unique purpose God has for me.
- ♦   I will reach out to other people.
- ♦   I will remember it is not who I am but Whose I am!
- ♦   I will daily thank the Lord for using me.

I read a touching story about a young man who was kidnapped from his home in Africa and taken to America on a slave ship. For months he experienced rotten food, disease, and death all around him—things that should have destroyed his heart and spirit. Yet, when it was time for him to be placed on a platform to be sold, this young man stood boldly with his chest out and his chin up. The crowd noticed quickly that he was different, and the slave trader explained, "This boy is the son of a king in Africa and he can't forget it."

We are daily surrounded by sin and death—the corruption of our culture, as well as the internal assault of a ruthless enemy. He is constantly reminding us of our past, our present, and our failures. Among all of this distraction, it is easy to become discouraged. It's easy to forget that we are children of the King!

God delights in helping His children overcome personal obstacles. He delights in enabling us, strengthening us, and equipping us for His glory. Friend, rejoice that you have a weakness, as long as that weakness is surrendered to His strength.

One thing is certain: As we are all aware of our personal obstacles, there is only one Person who can truly be credited with our successes—the Lord Jesus Christ. Serve in His strength, and rejoice to give Him the glory for what He accomplishes through you.

And, just in case you forgot…

> If God had a refrigerator, your picture would be on it.
> If God had a wallet, your photo would be in it.
> He sends you fresh flowers every spring and a sunrise
>   every morning.
> When you want to talk, He will listen.
> He could live anywhere in the universe and yet He
>   chose your heart.
> And that Christmas gift He sent you in Bethlehem?
> Face it, friend, He is crazy about you!
>   —Author Unknown

CHAPTER SEVEN

Balancing Your Family and Ministry

 *false balance is abomination to the LORD: but a just weight is his delight.*—Proverbs 11:1

When I was a freshman in high school, I had a P.E. class first hour (which was 7:30 AM)! We had over 1,000 students in our freshman class, so a large percentage of them would join students from the other grades for first hour P.E. each morning.

We were allowed to choose the sports we wanted to participate in; however, the seniors had first choice, juniors—second choice, sophomores—third choice, and, you guessed it, the freshmen had last choice!

Since our class was so large, most sports available to freshmen were those that would accommodate a lot of players—sports such as football and soccer.

My friend Diane and I did not like the large crowds, nor did we care for football or soccer, so we thought a good alternative would be the synchronized swimming class. The only thing we knew about synchronized swimming was that it was a small class with about twelve girls, and since we were required to shower at the end of the first hour period, why not go ahead and get wet anyway!

On the first day of class, it didn't take us long to find out that we were the only ones in the entire class who knew absolutely nothing about synchronized swimming! To this day, I believe that the only reason our teacher allowed us to stay in the class was that we kept her laughing the entire hour.

While the other ten students glided effortlessly across the water, Diane and I struggled to stay afloat! We paddled harder than anyone else, and our arms and legs flailed in every direction as we tried to keep from drowning. When class was over, the other girls walked out of the gym refreshed and ready for the day, but Diane and I were so exhausted we could barely walk to our next class!

Many of us live our lives like inexperienced swimmers, expending great amounts of energy in attempts to survive. We thrash our way from one circumstance to another, never seeming to have the strength to do the really important things in our lives. We are out of balance.

When I get out of balance, I feel as if I'm drowning—being pulled down by a huge octopus of details, demands, and emotions. I feel like I'm being pulled from one crisis to another, responding to the *urgent* instead of to the *important*. I struggle to get on top of my "to-do list" and don't even get close to my "*want* to-do list." I feel like a frazzled mess, and I have so little energy to get through my day. Does this sound familiar? Do you ever feel overwhelmed? Do you find yourself wishing you had just a couple more hours in your day? Have you lost your joy? Are you always coming up short and feeling exhausted? If your answer is "yes," you have experienced imbalance.

Most of us would agree that a tightrope walker has perfect balance, but in reality, he is just constantly making adjustments with every step he takes. A tightrope walker must constantly shift his weight to respond to all the outside forces that threaten his balance. In March, 1978, the great tightrope walker Karl Wallenda fell to his death—he had lost his balance. Losing our balance can kill us as well—it can kill our home, our ministry, our friendships, and our testimony.

Have you ever tripped and then turned to look at what you tripped on? That's what I would like for you to do now. What are you tripping on? What are you doing that is making your life unbalanced? Let's first identify the forces that threaten to knock us down or pull us under, and in the next chapter, we will explore some areas that will keep us on the rope or above the water.

Comparisons

The first force that pulls us down and knocks us off balance is that of comparison. Second Corinthians 10:12 says, *"For we dare not make ourselves of the number, or compare ourselves with some that commend themselves: but they measuring themselves by themselves, and comparing themselves among themselves, are not wise."* The two most common areas in which people compare themselves are through possessions and through achievements.

Possessions

Many times, we try to "keep up with the Joneses." But to keep up with others, we have to work longer hours, and with that, sacrifice family time, miss church, and pay a price we don't want to pay. In some cases, the wife will work outside the home to earn money to help pay for these possessions, and this means less time for family and a more hectic and fatigued family environment.

The root of this is covetousness, and the cure is contentment. The reward of contentment is balance! Your kids, your spouse, and your ministry will greatly benefit from a heart that refuses to compare in the area of possessions.

Achievements

When we focus on what others are doing and we try to do the same or better, we are focusing too much on achievements. We try to keep up with someone else's schedule or accomplishments—forgetting that God has given each of us different abilities, talents, and gifts, and forgetting that we may be in different stages of life with different demands or pressures.

For example, a mother with four small children at home will not have as much time to volunteer as a mother with grown children. If the younger mother compares herself to the other, she will fall short and feel like a failure. She could end up over-committing herself and robbing her children and home of what they need the most.

There's no "one size fits all" for standardizing your life, home, or ministry. The result of this comparison is that we end up not doing the will of God for our individual lives. Comparison keeps us from being who God designed us to be and traps us in failed attempts to be someone else! Comparing ourselves will cause us either to do more than what God wants us to do or to do less—both are disappointing to the Lord.

When we compare, most of us tend to exaggerate the other person's qualities and abilities while minimizing our own. If we are not careful, when we compare ourselves to others, we always come up short. On the opposite end of the spectrum, we might compare and then think more highly of ourselves, having a false self-confidence because we do more than the person next to us. In both cases, we put unnecessary pressure on ourselves, and we find ourselves out of balance.

> *For I say, through the grace given unto me, to every man that is among you, not to think of himself more highly than he ought to*

think; but to think soberly, according as God hath dealt to every
man the measure of faith.—ROMANS 12:3

Don't undermine your worth by comparing yourself with others. It is because we are different that each of us is special! I can have twenty people over on a Sunday for lunch while another woman has only two guests. One lady teaches a ladies' class, and another works in the nursery. When each is doing what the Lord wants, it is like comparing roses and lilies—both are beautiful and both are equally honoring to the Lord.

Women have been comparing themselves for a long time. I think of Mary and Martha in the New Testament. Martha started comparing what she was doing to what Mary was doing, and she went to Jesus to complain. But her comparison backfired. Jesus told Martha that Mary was doing that which was more needful.

Let us remember that each person—each ministry wife—is unique, with a specific God-given set of attributes and abilities. And all of us have areas where we can grow and improve. The bottom line is this: Ministry will look different on every person, and balance will look different for each person. We are individuals and therefore incomparable.

So, here is my challenge to you. Stop comparing yourself to others. Whether you think you fall short or not, accept your unique gifts, abilities, and callings as from God and for His glory. Comparison is like a prison—holding you from being God's unique servant and serving Him with your unique gifts. Surrender is the key to the prison. Yield to being the unique person God created you to be, and begin serving Him fully from your heart.

People Pleasing

The second thing that destroys balance in our lives is a desire to please people. Herbert Bayard Swope said, "I cannot give you the formula for success, but I can give you the formula for failure: try to please everyone." Attempting to please others all the time is an impossible task and a sure recipe for frustration. What makes some people happy one time won't make them happy the next. What pleases one person will anger another. It has been called the "disease to please."

People-pleasers cannot say "no." They try to do whatever they are asked, all the time, every time, giving no thought to whether they have the time, energy, ability, or desire. People-pleasers say "yes" when they really should say "no." They let others schedule their priorities or activities. They take criticism personally. They depend too much on compliments to feel good. They try too hard to be nice and to meet everyone's expectations all the time. The consequence of this type of life is imbalance.

Don't misunderstand, there is nothing wrong with being nice or helpful. There's nothing wrong with having an accommodating attitude as long as it is for the right reasons. People-pleasers fear people. They fear rejection or guilt. They fear not being accepted or well-liked. They fear letting others down. They operate out of guilt rather than conviction. Guilt should not be a reason for doing something, but conviction should!

Proverbs 29:25 says, *"The fear of man bringeth a snare: but whoso putteth his trust in the LORD shall be safe."* When we try to meet everyone's expectations, we will inevitably fail. When that happens, we feel guilty, so we try harder and harder. We become obsessed because of a constant sense of obligation.

Life will always be full of expectations—your own and others'. How you respond to these expectations will determine how worn out and out of balance you will become. The key, of course, is to stop letting others control you through their expectations. Instead, listen to God, trust Him, obey Him, and be guided by His expectations.

Scripture reminds us to please God, not people.

And whatsoever we ask, we receive of him, because we keep his commandments, and do those things that are pleasing in his sight.—1 JOHN 3:22

But as we were allowed of God to be put in trust with the gospel, even so we speak; not as pleasing men, but God, which trieth our hearts.—1 THESSALONIANS 2:4

Then Peter and the other apostles answered and said, We ought to obey God rather than men.—ACTS 5:29

Are you a people-pleaser? Do you know how to say "no" kindly and politely with a clear conscience and a pure heart? Do you find yourself hostage to the expectations or demands of others? God desires for you to be free from that kind of guilt and frustration. There is something wonderful about serving God and serving people as unto the Lord. Stop living to please people and start living to please Christ alone. Be willing to say "no" to the demands or priorities of people when doing so allows you to say "yes" to God and to His priorities.

Personal Expectations

Perfectionism (or self-imposed expectations) is the third factor that leads the way to imbalance in our Christian lives. Perfectionists are hard workers and can be very meticulous in the way they get things done. Sometimes they will spend more time on a project than is needed, and often they are so worn out by their own expectations that they fail to do anything at all. If you are a perfectionist, here are a few principles to help you fight perfectionism:

+ Admit that perfection is impossible.
+ Set realistic and reachable goals.
+ Aim for excellence, not perfection.

Just like people-pleasers, perfectionists must follow the Holy Spirit's leading. Learn to set aside your own preferences, agenda, and expectations, and ask God to give you a sensitivity to listen to His still small voice as He guides you through your daily routines.

Over-Commitment

Over-commitment is the fourth cause of imbalance. An Italian proverb says, "He who begins many things finishes but few." If you find yourself beginning many things but finishing few, this is a good indication that you are over-committed and out of balance.

Wishing for just two more hours a day is a revealing signal that we have taken on more than God ever desired for us to do. Over-commitment is exhausting, and it literally makes balance impossible because "urgent" issues will almost always crowd out those that are more important. Over-commitment causes us to hear only the loud noises of urgency and immediate crisis. It deafens us to the quiet and highly important needs of our families, our hearts, our husbands, and our ministries.

Most of us overcrowd our schedules because *we want to.* The praise and admiration we receive from family and friends gives us a temporary feeling of satisfaction—it's a wonderful ego boost that makes us feel valuable, important, and significant. This leads us on a quest for admiration, which causes us to unconsciously commit to things that are really not important. We should actively and deliberately choose how we invest our lives, and our choices should not be based upon what will most immediately gratify our ego or need for affirmation. Our choices should be based upon the leading and purposes of God—that which is truly important, whether it is urgent or not.

Are you over-committed? When you look at your schedule, do you see more than you can possibly do? A better question is this: When you pillow your head at night, do you have the inner peace of a clear conscience, knowing that you invested your time and energy into the most important priorities of your life that day? If not, then it's time to say "no" to some things. It's time to take some things off the schedule so that more important priorities can have their rightful place. This is honoring to God, so go for it, and don't feel guilty!

Discontentment

Balance is also often threatened by discontentment. We want to do it all and do it all now. Remember there are *seasons* in life and in ministry. When my children were young, they were my primary focus, and rightfully so. This does not mean that I did not have a ministry; I was very involved in ministry. It simply means that I purposely focused my energies into caring and nurturing them *first*. I knew they would not be small forever, and I would never get this time with them again.

There is a flip side to this as well; we *are* talking about balance, right? There is a danger that we can be "content to do nothing"—to choose *not* to serve the Lord and then to use excuses to justify our choices. For example, having small children is not an excuse for not serving God or for not being actively involved in His work. This is not contentment nor is it balance. It is *imbalance*. What should not change in our quest to find balance is our commitment to *both* family and church.

As my children have grown and the seasons of my life have changed, I have had the freedom to expand into other areas of ministry, always remembering to refocus and adjust in the pursuit for balance. Through this, God taught me to accept and be content with the season in which He has me. To desire another life-season or to try to "do it all now" would be nothing more than discontentment. This is a journey, so stop askingn "are we there yet," and start enjoying the trip!

Philippians 4:11 reminds us to be content in every season, *"Not that I speak in respect of want: for I have learned, in whatsoever state I am, therewith to be content."* Don't fall into the trap of thinking "tomorrow, life will be better." Sometimes we stew in discontentment over today, while we think things like this: "The kids will be older; they will do more for themselves; I won't have to worry as much; or we will have more money."

That may not happen! Life may or may not get better. In reality, it just gets *different*! I don't want to wait for a better tomorrow and miss out on today! I would rather make today everything that God wants it to be. I would rather joyfully embrace where God has placed me for His glory and make the most of the moments I have right now. I want to make the most of life's irretrievable moments, *now*! I desire to live in the present.

One way to get rid of discontentment is to be thankful. First Thessalonians 5:18 tells us, *"In every thing give thanks: for this is the will of God in Christ Jesus concerning you."*

For example, I love spending time with my husband! In fact, I think quality time is the predominant of my "five love languages." I would love to spend all my time with him, but that's not realistic. We would be out of balance if we tried it! So, instead of becoming annoyed with my husband because he doesn't spend all of his time with me, I look forward to and am thankful for the time I *do* get to spend with him.

Enjoy and appreciate your family, even if they don't pick up their dirty socks or put away their toys. Be thankful for ministry, even though it's not a nine-to-five job. Be thankful for every opportunity to serve Christ.

A true key to finding and maintaining contentment is to deliberately choose to be thankful for each and every blessing of God! My husband has said many times, "The foundation of gratitude is the expectation of nothing." I guess that means that the foundation of discontentment is the expectation of things! When we allow ourselves to harbor unmet expectations, we quickly slip into discontentment, imbalance, and frustration in our lives.

Time Wasters and Pointless Activity

Another thing that can get us out of balance in a hurry is wasting time on futile activities. Benjamin Franklin said, "He that is good for making excuses is seldom good for anything else." And Gabriel Meurier said, "He who excuses himself, accuses himself."

The simple fact is that many times we are out of balance because we are wasting time on meaningless activity. Some common time wasters would be:

- Not planning your day properly
- Careless mistakes that take time to fix
- Putting something off until a later, more stressful time
- Not listening to instructions
- Lack of self-discipline
- Excessive television or computer usage
- Idle phone chatting
- Sleeping in too much

Maybe you were planning to sit down to watch just a few minutes of the news and then found yourself still in front of the TV hours later. Remember that quick phone call that turned into twenty minutes of chatter? Time is precious, and we must use the time God has given to us for the things that matter most to Him.

Decide that you will discipline your life and use your time wisely. Say "no" to time wasters and choose to invest your life rather than spend it!

Circumstances Beyond Our Control

Another cause of imbalance is the desire to control our circumstances. In the ministry, this just isn't possible.

Having a heart for God is the key to having a balanced perspective in life. We must understand that His ministry is "people work," and people take time and energy. The ministry is more than a job; it's a passion for people. This means that ministry is as unpredictable as the needs, crises, and circumstances of the people that we serve. If you are going to stay in balance in ministry, you need to have a high degree of flexibility. You cannot control every moment of every day—that's God's job. Flexibility is a willingness to bend with the leading of the Holy Spirit, and that goes both ways—for family and for ministry. Stay flexible; it is imperative for keeping your balance.

Trying to take charge of all events in life only leads to frustration and despair. Accept the realities of life in the ministry. Ministry will sometimes require our husbands to be called away unexpectedly. Your goal should not be to steal him back from ministry but to help him find a balance between home and work.

Someone said that "life has a life of its own." That is so true! Babies spit up on you just as you're ready to walk out the door, a button pops off a shirt the one day you're running late, a pot boils over as company walks in the door, and the list goes on. So when the circumstances change, readjust to achieve the balance. Be willing to flex with God and accept what He ordains—that which is only in His control. Always be mindful that circumstances outside of my control are still in God's control. Any circumstance out of my control must be the will of God for my life.

Failing To Understand Acceptance in Christ

The last thing that can knock us off balance is failure to grasp our acceptance in Christ. If we have an improper understanding of who we are from God's perspective, we will often be discouraged and find our lives out of balance.

God made each of us, and we are precious in His sight. Ephesians 1:6 says, *"To the praise of the glory of his grace, wherein he hath made us accepted in the beloved."* When we learn to see ourselves as God sees us—forgiven and free from sin—then we are truly free to drop our burdens of guilt over not being good enough or talented enough or strong enough. In the light of His acceptance, we can truly become all that He created us to be. All the "doing" in the world will never be enough to earn us the kind of consistent significance that we long for in life. God alone provides this, and we must seek our significance from Him. Our "doing" does not define us; our Heavenly Father defines us and accepts us fully in His love and grace.

Are you struggling to find acceptance from everywhere and everyone but God? If so, you are empty, and you are on a search that will never end. Why not end your search right now at the foot of the cross of Christ? Why not find rest in the fact that you are most precious in God's sight, and you are very much a work in progress by His grace?

Imbalance comes into our lives for a great variety of reasons, which we have seen above, and when we are out of balance, all of life can be a confusing, frustrating mess. Maybe you can identify with the things we've talked about in this chapter. If so, then let's press on and discover the things that can bring balance back!

CHAPTER EIGHT

Bringing Balance Back

So, are you tired of living out of balance? If you are, I can certainly relate! Let's consider what we can do to bring balance back into our lives and ministries. Here are some key principles to developing and maintaining a healthy balance.

Surrender to and Stay in the Center of God's Will

First, we need to stay in the center of God's will. As an elementary student, one of my favorite recess activities was to play on the merry-go-round. All the kids would grab one of the iron handles and run for all they were worth. Then, when the merry-go-round was traveling as fast as it could, we would all jump on. If you were sitting close to the outside, you would have to hold on with all your might, because it was easy to get thrown off into the bark. The kids who sat close to the middle very seldom were thrown off or lost their balance. The center of the merry-go-round was the safest place to be.

Christ needs to be at the center of your life. Everything else stems from your relationship with Him. Colossians 1:16–17 says, *"For by him were all things created, that are in heaven, and that are in earth, visible and invisible, whether they be thrones, or dominions, or principalities, or powers: all things were created by him, and for him: And he is before all things, and by him all things consist."*

The earth balances in space because God is holding it there. Without God, our world would spin out of control. If your life is spinning out of control, it is because Christ is not in the center, holding things together, and it is because *we* are not centered in His will.

This may sound counter-productive to the message of this chapter, but the goal is not balance. The goal is submission to God! The goal is to bring every area of life into agreement with God's will, for only then will your heart experience His peace and your life experience His presence and His guiding touch.

Friend, if you find yourself struggling to hang on as your life seems to spin wildly out of control, surrender control to God. Submit to His perfect will and purpose to make Him the very center of your life.

> *Wherefore be ye not unwise, but understanding what the will of the Lord is.*—Ephesians 5:17

It is only as we make Christ first and subject everything else in our lives to Him that we experience a truly balanced life—a life where every role has its proper place and all the roles are properly connected to one another and to Christ. A major part of keeping your balance is being faithful where God has placed you and being obedient to the things He has given you to do.

In the synchronized swimming class, the experienced students had learned how to allow the water to be their friend, give them buoyancy, and hold up most of their weight. Those like me tend to fight the water and struggle for survival.

This is the very principle that Jesus shared in Matthew 11:28–30, when He said, *"Come unto me, all ye that labour and are heavy laden, and I will give you rest. Take my yoke upon you, and learn of me; for I am meek and lowly in heart: and ye shall find rest unto your souls. For my yoke is easy, and my burden is light."* Jesus promises that His yoke is easy and His burden is light. He does not want us to fight every battle on our own or feel as if we must constantly struggle from event to event. When He becomes the center of our lives and when we submit wholly and fully to His yoke, we find His strength and enabling. At the center of His will is balance and rest. Outside of His yoke (or His will) is frustration, struggle, and imbalance.

Often, we take too many burdens upon ourselves, both physically and emotionally, and it really boils down to a subtle form of rebellion against the will of God. Are you struggling against His yoke? Maybe as you read this, you find yourself resisting God's call in your life or even resisting your husband's ministry. This resistance will bring great exasperation to your life, and I urge you to let go of the struggle and embrace His yoke for you. Let me encourage you today to rest in the Lord—to surrender sincerely and completely to His will for your life. Cast your care upon Him because He truly does care for you!

Spend Time with the Lord Daily

I worked my way through college by being a waitress, and over time I learned how to balance quite a few plates on one arm. Sometimes I would try to carry too many plates at once and could feel that I was losing balance. In those moments, I would immediately remove one or two of the plates to keep the rest from falling.

When we are feeling out of balance in our Christian life, occasionally we need to remove a plate or two. It is in choosing which plate that we often make our mistake. We usually give up the plate that doesn't cry out to us—like personal devotions! Sometimes the quiet plates are the most important plates.

Never let go of the time that you spend with your Lord. Matthew 6:33 says, *"But seek ye first the kingdom of God, and his righteousness; and all these things shall be added unto you."*

Every time I have flown in an airplane, the flight attendant has said, "If you are flying with small children, please put the mask on yourself first *and then* assist the children." Before we can balance all of our roles and responsibilities, we must take care of our *own* spiritual well being.

Long ago, there was a lighthouse keeper in charge of keeping the oil light burning so sailors could safely navigate along a dangerous stretch of the Atlantic coastline. Once a month he received a supply of oil. Since the lighthouse was near a coastal village, the lighthouse keeper had frequent visitors, and most of them needed to borrow a little oil. One woman needed oil to keep her family warm. Another guest needed oil for his lamps. Other visitors also had what seemed to be genuine needs, and the kind lighthouse keeper tried to meet them all.

Toward the end of one month a terrible storm hit the rocky coastline. The faithful lighthouse keeper was at his position tending the lamp so ships could safely pass, but before dawn, while the storm still raged and the ships were being tossed by terrifying winds and crashing waves, the oil ran out and the lighthouse went dark.

A woman in ministry is often called on to be a spiritual help to others in the church. We give a little here and a little there, and if we are not careful, we will not replenish our spiritual energy on a daily basis. Then, when a sudden storm enters our lives and the great need for spiritual reserve hits us, we may be empty.

The principle here is simple, yet so vital. You cannot give and give endlessly. You must also restore. You must renew and refresh in the presence of the Lord. Your time with God is that vital, replenishing lifeline you need as you serve your Lord, your husband, your family, and your church. Without it, you will, like the lighthouse keeper, eventually have nothing left to offer.

Set Boundaries and Establish Values

Jeremiah 29:11 says, *"For I know the thoughts that I think toward you, saith the LORD, thoughts of peace, and not of evil, to give you an expected end."* God has a plan for each one of us. He has saved us for a reason and has a purpose for us to fulfill in life. To fulfill His purpose, we must establish biblical values which will determine our daily priorities. Priorities keep you focused and balanced on a weekly and daily basis, but biblical values define your priorities for *all* of life.

Setting priorities is not about choosing between what is good and what is bad. Nor are priorities about what is godly and what is worldly. Setting life's priorities is about choosing between what is good and what is best. This is actually "doing the will of the Lord" as opposed to "doing good things for the Lord."

Consider this thought: Do you understand your purpose in life? Has God clearly impressed on your heart through His call, His Word, and through your husband's leadership what His purpose is for you? If not, then I challenge you to define this clearly in your heart before God. Identify, accept, and embrace that yoke that we talked about earlier.

Once you discover your purpose, write it out. Put your life's priorities on paper—and then on the calendar. After this, put boundaries into place.

My husband and I have established some of these boundaries. For example, from past experience, we knew there would be plenty of invitations to parties like Tupperware, Pampered Chef, or Home Interiors within the church. They are a lot of fun, and I enjoy going to them. But, I also know that I could quickly and easily find myself attending some sort of home party every single week. This would obviously compete with my God-given priorities. So, we decided that it would be best to not attend any. That's our boundary. This way no one gets her feelings hurt if I attend one and not another. I always ask to see a catalog, and if there is something I need, I get it. This makes the hostess happy and my family happy. Boundaries can also be set for children's slumber parties, fellowship times, Saturday night activities, and birthday celebrations. For each family or each couple, the boundaries will be different. You must be willing to talk about these boundaries, pray about them, and seek God's wisdom in creating them. Then, let your God-given boundaries help you make the right decisions to stay in balance.

Maintain a Weekly Schedule

Another step in maintaining balance is to schedule your week. Psalm 90:12 says, "*So teach us to number our days, that we may apply our hearts unto wisdom.*" Staying in balance means deliberately scheduling things that are important to us. Nothing is going to happen unless you make it happen, and that includes time with your kids, your husband, and your Lord! It is too easy to let life sweep you along and to allow your daily schedule to be filled with urgent, insignificant things.

If you are not deliberate in planning, time will drift, and life will "just happen." Evaluate where you spend your time and see if your actual *living* lines up with what you say are your priorities. For a good balance, assign your time and energy based on your priorities and biblical values.

Based on my priorities, here are some of the things that I make sure are on the calendar.

Time with the Lord

I must spend time with God, renewing my strength, resting in Him, and walking in His wisdom. I must read His Word, talk with Him in prayer, and meditate on His precepts for my life.

Family time
I must make sure the entire family stays connected. Though this gets harder as my kids have grown, we still make family nights, time together, and family fun a real priority in our home. Over the years, my husband has made this a priority as well, and the whole family greatly benefits because of it.

Date nights
No matter how busy or demanding ministry can be for both me and my husband, our marriage must remain strong. This cannot happen if we don't spend time together. I thank the Lord for a husband who has made this a priority as well.

Date days or trips
Several times a year we find it helpful for our marriage if we go away together for a few days and nights. These have become some of our most cherished memories. We read books on marriage together, pray, walk, talk, and truly cherish these times together. It's not about spending money or being entertained. It's just about spending time together strengthening our relationship.

Soulwinning
Every week I must find time to visit, share the Gospel, and reach out to the lost. This is the heart of God and the very reason He has placed us in the ministry. I may go a week or so without winning someone to Christ, but I don't want it to be because I haven't tried.

Hospitality
It is necessary to schedule time to nurture and love God's people. Usually, these are people that the Lord has laid on our hearts through various ministry outlets. Hospitality is a big priority with us, and we decided a long time ago that it *will* be on the schedule.

Rest

We can't go without it! Isn't it amazing how God designed us to need a certain amount of sleep every twenty-four hours? You may need more or less than I do, but we're basically all in the same boat. There's nothing spiritual about not resting, and sometimes the only way to get rest is to plan it. If you get rest when you've scheduled to do so, don't feel guilty.

Your list may differ from mine, but these are the things that are a part of God's "yoke" for me. If they don't get scheduled in my week, they are not a priority in my life, which means I'm living out of God's will.

Being flexible is very important, which is why I say to schedule your week rather than your day. Looking at a seven-day portion gives you a better perspective as your daily schedule sometimes changes. Emergencies, phone calls, visitors, and interruptions are part of life and a vital part of ministry—so expect them. But, don't let these things discourage you from making a weekly schedule altogether.

Somebody said, "If you're going to hit the target, you've got to take aim." My husband often says, "He who aims at nothing hits it every time!" If we want to make time for the important things in life, we have to schedule it.

Seek Counsel

Sometimes, we need a little help in our quest for balance. Most likely there is someone within your reach who has been down this road before and who could give you some great advice. Do you know someone who can provide honest, godly counsel and someone who you will listen to? For me, that person is my husband. When my life starts to take on more than I can handle, my husband will let me know that I am getting a little out of balance, and he will help me to get back on track.

Proverbs 11:14, "*Where no counsel is, the people fall: but in the multitude of counsellors there is safety.*" Counselors will provide perspective. When I'm overwhelmed, it's easy to become blinded to my options. Sometimes, the answer is right in front of my face, and I don't even see it! It's like the old saying, "You can't see the forest for the trees."

A faithful counselor will offer accountability and honest perspective. A godly advisor will sincerely desire to know how you are doing at prioritizing and will suggest a biblical course of correction when life is out of balance.

Finally, a counselor provides encouragement. When we get out of balance, we can easily get wrapped up in negativity, and a godly voice will bring us back to the yoke and help us maintain a right spirit.

Simplify and Share

Sometimes we need to simplify and remember to share the load to help achieve a healthy balance. Delegating tasks and responsibilities is a wonderful way to keep your schedule balanced, not to mention that it is a great way to mentor others. Teaching and encouraging someone else may indeed take extra effort on your part, but only at the beginning. For instance, teaching your children how to help you clean the house or host a guest will take more time initially, but soon, your children will be developing valuable skills and helping *you*! Someone said, "As we become more effective, we begin to create balance, which makes us even more effective!"

Take a look at what's on your plate and ask yourself this question: "Who could help with this?" The Lord has probably already surrounded you with people who are skilled, interested, and available. Don't rob them of the blessing!

Stay Focused

A big component of balance is staying focused. If you were to balance on a tightrope, the first and most important thing you must do is to fix your eyes onto something in front of you that isn't moving. This is usually an object at the end of the rope on which you are walking or a point on the wall ahead. Focusing helps you to balance and also stops you from looking down at your feet, which makes you fall forward in fear. As Christians, we need to fix our eyes on the Lord who never moves. He is always the same. As I mentioned earlier, when our eyes are on others or on ourselves, we will fall. Psalm 25:15 says, *"Mine eyes are ever toward the LORD; for he shall pluck my feet out of the net."*

Not only do we need to stay focused on the Lord, but we also need to focus on the task at hand. We need to give one hundred percent of our effort in whatever task we do, as unto the Lord.

It's funny how we have a tendency to wish we were doing something else. For example, during the school year I can't wait for summer. When summer comes, I can't wait for school to start. Does that sound familiar? Do you find that, at times, your mind seems unfocused—out of control, racing off in many directions at once?

It is very difficult to concentrate on the task at hand while we are worried or thinking of something else. When we are focused, we will do more in less time and do it more effectively. Because we are able to concentrate on the job before us, we can be more effective and efficient. We can do an amazing amount of work when we are focused.

So when you are at church, give one hundred percent—focus. Don't be the last one to arrive and the first to leave. Decide, "If I am going to be at church, I will give one hundred percent! I will stay focused on the preaching of God's Word, serve where I can, fellowship with other Christians, and give a smiling word of encouragement to as many people as I can."

When you are with your husband, give him one hundred percent of your attention. That's what we did when we dated, isn't it? When we were together, we gave each other our undivided attention! Now that years have gone by, be very careful to not waste the time you do get together focusing on finances, problems, or kids. Focus on each other!

The same concept holds true with your family. Time spent with your family is always precious, so when you have time together, give your family your undivided attention. Kids know if you are paying attention to them or if your mind is a million miles away. Even small children know!

When my son, Larry, was very little, he would work to get our attention. If he felt that we weren't listening, he would climb into our laps and grab our face in his little hands—forcing our eyes to connect with his. It was cute, but it was also a real indicator that, even as a toddler, he knew if we were truly giving him the focused attention he deserved!

Sometimes people allow their family and ministry priorities to get out of focus. I've often heard it said that parents in the ministry have to guard their family from the burdens and busyness of ministry. That statement makes me feel uneasy. I don't want to "guard" my family against the Lord or His work. It doesn't make sense to me that God would call us to something that is dangerous to our family! In reality, that type of talk is a smokescreen. We don't need to protect our children in the Lord's work, and we are out of focus if we think this way! We need to guard them against our *own* bad decisions. The ministry never ruined anyone's children, but bad parental choices have.

Truthfully, if we want to guard our families, why not guard them from some of the other major sources of distractions that attack them, like TV, PlayStation games, hobbies, internet, wrong friends, extracurricular activities, and a myriad of other "things" that grab our attention away from our priorities? It's amazing that sometimes, in our minds, the ministry can be the "danger" while all these other distractions are left alone. Decide to provide your family with the focus and attention they need in areas such as these.

So, keep your heart fixed on the roles and responsibilities at hand! Don't let tension, confusion, frustration, and even spiritual defeat get in the way of balancing ministry and home. Ask God for a fresh perspective and a purposeful focus *today*!

> Lost yesterday, somewhere between sunrise and sunset,
> two golden hours, each set with sixty diamond minutes.
> No reward is offered, for they are gone forever.

Be Sensitive to the Direction You Are Leaning

It's hard to maintain balance. Most of the time we are probably tipped too far one way or the other. Humor me for a minute, and try this little exercise. Stand up and raise one foot off the ground. Notice that even though you can remain in place, you are making continual adjustments. That is how we will maintain balance. Just as a tightrope walker has to remain sensitive to the way he is leaning, so must we, as Christian wives, be sensitive to the way we are leaning.

For example, when my family is on vacation, we are focused totally on the family! We are not heavily involved in ministry at all. Remember, we are still Christians even on vacation. We go to church, we share the Gospel—in fact, some of our fondest memories are of those we led to the Lord while on vacation. But we don't do a lot of counseling, preaching (my husband, that is), and other things that would take away from family time. You could say we are purposefully leaning heavily on the family side.

Then there are times throughout the year when our calendar is full with church ministry. In the fall season, we have a big outreach program and Harvest Time campaign. During these months, we are leaning heavily on the ministry side—and again, it's on purpose. We may go soulwinning with a member of our family, eat together a couple times as a family, but our focus is on getting the Gospel message out into the community.

The danger comes when we stop making continual adjustments to remain balanced or when we stop being sensitive to the direction of our "lean."

When the kids were younger, we took them to see a small town circus. It was pretty "hokey," but they did have one family that did some good balancing acts. One, in particular, was when the father balanced a chair on his head as his daughter sat on it! I was amazed! I watched as he performed this balancing act and noticed how he continually made adjustments—he never stood still. He never stopped!

As soon as we stop balancing, we will fall—we'll be out of balance. Remember our standing-on-one-leg exercise? Standing on one leg requires our attention, some adjustment, and recalibration. If someone bumped you or a strong wind came by while you were standing on one leg? Could you maintain your balance? It would require a more dramatic adjustment, but you might be able to do it. But if the outside force was too strong to maintain your balance and you had to put both feet on the ground to stay up, would you then be able to get back up and continue balancing on one foot? Of course! So if you find that you're being periodically knocked off balance, it is not permanent unless you choose to do nothing about it.

The principle here is never to quit trying to establish balance in your life. Let's continue to strive for balance every day of our lives.

In conclusion to these thoughts, consider this final question: Why do I want to maintain a balanced life? Friend, there is only one good answer. It should be because you want to finish your course in the way that will please God! A balanced lifestyle enables us not only to *begin* well, but also, and far more importantly, to *end* well. As we maintain spiritual balance and stability, let's remember to give God the glory continually!

> *Whether therefore ye eat, or drink, or whatsoever ye do, do all to the glory of God.*—1 CORINTHIANS 10:31

CHAPTER NINE

From the Glass House to the Greenhouse

We've probably all heard it said, "The preacher's family lives in a glass house." And though this comment is typically stated in a negative tone, it may be true. The pastor's family *is* sometimes watched with a critical eye. But I propose to you today that the "glass house" environment doesn't have to be a negative experience!

My dad had a green thumb! He loved to spend time working in his yard in San Jose, California, and he took particular care of his garden. Neighbors would often come by to admire the fruit of his labor. They would ask advice on how to grow their gardens so they could reap a plentiful harvest.

The garden required a lot of time, effort, and patience on his part. He would often take a tiny seed, plant it in a little cup of good soil, and place that cup in a shed with big windows that allowed plenty of sunlight. Daily, he would nurture that tiny seed until little sprouts—and then, finally, a plant—appeared. The small shed protected the seedlings from the cold and other harmful elements. Eventually, the plant would grow strong enough to be planted outside.

That shed was a greenhouse! The official definition of a greenhouse is "a structure, primarily of glass, in which temperature and humidity can be controlled for the cultivation or protection of plants." Though we could see *inside* the shed, its contents were being protected from the harmful, *outside* elements.

As a parent who has raised children in the "glass house" of a pastor's home, may I encourage you to change your perspective? Turn your glass house into a greenhouse of godly growth for your family! Focus on the good that comes from a secure, protected environment, and even allow the pressure of the watchful eye of others to add to your family's development and betterment. Ask God to help you create in your home an atmosphere conducive to spiritual growth, even when the outside elements are hostile towards your children. Pray for a home that will sustain even the most delicate and fragile of tender seedlings—your children—until they are strong and healthy enough in the Lord to be in the world.

In Bible college, I heard stories about "PKs" who turned away from the Lord. Somewhere along the line, they decided that they didn't want anything to do with God or church. At the time, that thought terrified me! I wanted to serve the Lord with no reservations, but I didn't want to lose my family in the process. Other times I would hear the phrase, "He lost his family while trying to save the world." What a sad testimony! (And unscriptural, I might add.) Life in ministry does not have to be that way. You can have a happy family while serving in ministry. But it's a choice! Will you choose the negative glass house approach, or by God's grace, will you determine to make your home a spiritual greenhouse for His glory?

I've always loved the story of Moses and his family. I love how God used this family to protect their son *and* save a nation! I am greatly encouraged by the fact that we serve the same God today—

a God who still possesses the power and provides the wisdom we need to raise godly children in the ministry. We do not have to lose our children while we attempt to save the world!

Our Christian school hosts a fine arts competition each year. When our oldest daughter, Danielle, was in the eleventh grade, she entered the Bible teaching portion of the competition. Being that she was in other areas of competition that were scheduled around the same time, she was quite frazzled and in a big hurry when she got up to teach. She was teaching on Jochebed in the first person.

She started, "Hello, boys and girls, my name is Ichabod." Danielle realized by the way my daughter Kristine and I were laughing that she must have said something wrong. So, a little flustered, she started over, "Hello, boys and girls, my name is Ichabod!" More laughter.

She started over three times before Kristine and I could control our laughter enough to whisper to her that she was saying "Ichabod" instead of "Jochebed." Suffice it to say, the glory had departed!

We (including Danielle) have laughed over that episode many times. But in all seriousness, I don't want "Ichabod" written over the door of my home!

Trusting God with Your Children

If Jochebed kept a journal or a diary, I wonder if it would read something like this:

Journal: My heart is overwhelmed. Today Pharaoh ruled that all male Hebrew babies will be placed in the Nile. I wonder if this baby will be a boy. The Lord knows what is ahead, and I will have to trust in Him.

Jochebed trusted God, and though Proverbs 3:5 was not yet written, she obeyed its command: *"Trust in the LORD with all thine heart; and lean not unto thine own understanding."*

When it comes to parenting, we must trust God and not ourselves. Here are some verses I have claimed while rearing my children in a perverse and wicked world:

+ Job 13:15 says, *"Though he slay me, yet will I trust in him: but I will maintain mine own ways before him."* Many Christians change their direction for the Lord when they become parents rather than maintaining their own ways before Him because it is right!

+ Psalm 56:11 says, *"In God have I put my trust: I will not be afraid what man can do unto me."*

+ Psalm 62:8 exhorts us, *"Trust in him at all times; ye people, pour out your heart before him: God is a refuge for us. Selah."* (Many times I have spent the night pouring out my heart to the Lord because I want to do the right thing as a parent.)

+ Psalm 146:3 warns us, *"Put not your trust in princes, nor in the son of man, in whom there is no help."* (Nor in Dr. Spock, nor in any other popular psychologist of the day.)

Jochebed trusted God in four aspects of parenting:

First, she trusted God with the circumstances. The events surrounding Moses' birth were not an easy pill to swallow for this family. When Moses was born, Jochebed did not throw her arms in the air and say, "Oh well, I trusted God and look what happened." She simply chose to respond differently!

If we can't change the circumstances, then we should change the way we respond to them, just as Jochebed did. Too often, we trust God to only change the circumstance instead of trusting Him to change us *in* the circumstance. If you are currently in a situation over which you have no control, trust God! Thank Him for the opportunity to prove Him and grow closer to Him.

Second, she trusted God with her child. In addition to trusting God with our circumstances, we must also learn to trust God with our children. Don't ever forget that, first and foremost, our children belong to the Lord. When we recognize this truth of ownership, it is much easier to trust God with our offspring.

We often think that it is so hard to leave our children in God's hands, yet I am thankful that I've never had to leave my baby in a basket in a crocodile infested river! We can learn a lot about trust from the example God gives us in Jochebed.

When our first child was born, we went a little overboard in protecting her. At the hospital, if my husband wanted to see Danielle, he had to put on a hospital gown and wear a surgical mask. So when we took Danielle home two days later, if anyone wanted to see or hold her, my husband made them wear a hospital gown and a surgical mask—no kidding! He even sprayed a few guests with Lysol. If it was good for the hospital, it was good for home.

A few months later, it started to get cold outside. Again, we did everything we knew to keep her safe and free from any of those horrible germs that could invade her body. One night I noticed she was developing a cough and seemed to have difficulty breathing, so we rushed her to the emergency room. By the time the doctor saw us, Danielle was sleeping soundly, no coughing, no difficulty breathing, so the doctor sent us home.

For the next four nights it was like déjà vu. Danielle appeared sick until we saw the doctor, and then she was fine! We saw the same doctor each night and finally on the fifth night the light came on. He asked if we kept the heater on in the apartment. I said proudly, "Of course!" I didn't want Danielle to kick off her blanket and catch a cold, so I turned the heater up as high as it would go. I smiled.

Next, the doctor asked if we noticed how she did better once in the cool air on the way to the hospital. My smile turned to a blank look. The doctor lectured me on how the heat was the problem and instructed me not to keep it set so high. Now I was crying.

I felt terrible! Here I was trying so hard to protect my little girl, and now *I* was the cause of the problem. I realized I could not maintain a perfectly sterile environment. I could do my best, but ultimately it was God who protected her. From that day forward, I began trusting God in a new way with my child.

I continued to make several small choices as a result of this one decision to trust God with my children. For instance, I realized it was okay to put my kids in the nursery. It seems as though many parents have adopted the thinking that all germs live in the church nursery; therefore, their children are not allowed there. I know of moms who refuse to put their babies in the church nursery, yet they will take them to the grocery store and let them suck on the cart handles (yuck!). Of course, I am not advocating such things as taking sick babies to church, but it *is* important to have our children and our families in church on a regular basis. Don't allow your lack of trust in God to keep your children safe and healthy hinder their or your spiritual growth! Truthfully, I enjoyed the few hours my babies were in the nursery each week. Knowing they were taken care of gave me the freedom to fellowship with others and more importantly, to hear the preaching of God's Word.

As your children grow, learn to trust the God-given authority in their lives. God knows who your children's teachers, youth pastors, and principals will be. Even when an authority figure disappoints you or makes a decision differently than you would have preferred, God is still all-knowing. He can work *all things* together for good, including things related to your children! Support those who have authority over your children, and work with them in bringing up your children for God.

There will come a time as your children continue to grow when you must "cut the apron strings" and begin to let them go. I can imagine how very difficult it must have been for Jochebed to take her hands off of that basket and to leave Miriam there to watch Moses.

Perhaps the most difficult part of our parenting is that the job ends (at least as we know it)! It is as if you are constantly working yourself *out* of a job! A parent/child relationship is different from other relationships. It doesn't merely *grow* (as do most relationships); it *transitions*! I am in that transition time right now, as I have begun to experience what I pray will be many wonderful years of knowing my children also as co-laborers together with the Lord.

It is very difficult for some parents when their kids start to leave home. (I am currently in this stage of life, so the message of this principle is ringing loud and clear to *me*!) My prayer is that, even at this point, I will not intentionally or unintentionally hinder my children from finding God's will for their lives. Like any other mother, I would love nothing more than for them to live near (not *with*!) me for the rest of my life, but I accept the fact that this may not be God's will for them. Whether it be choosing a college or going to the mission field, I want God's will for their lives more than anything else!

You can finish this statement I'm sure: "Our kids are safer on the mission field in the will of God than they would be under our wing and outside the will of God." I wholeheartedly believe the truth of that simple phrase.

One day our children will have families of their own. They will be responsible for themselves, and we might be tempted to think that we no longer need to trust God with them. But trusting God never stops—even when dealing with our children! Believe it or not, we will eventually see our grown children doing things differently than we would! For example, twenty years ago, we were told to have our babies sleep on their stomachs, because the doctors warned of the possibility of choking. Now, doctors tell parents *not* to let their kids sleep on their stomachs because they could suffocate! In situations like these, you'll need to continue to trust God and give advice only when asked!

Third, she trusted God for wisdom. I pray my life's verse back to God nearly every day. It's Jeremiah 33:3, *"Call unto me, and I will answer thee, and shew thee great and mighty things, which thou knowest not."* Frequently, I find myself asking God to show me something great and mighty that I don't know in regards to parenting. I need His wisdom.

Clearly, each child is unique. I have four children, and they are all completely different. Most of the time, I feel like I need four different parenting strategies! So, I regularly ask the Lord to give me the discernment to know how to deal with each one individually. I need wisdom to know when to be quiet, when to keep talking, when to discipline, and when to show grace!

Here are the verses I claim for getting the much needed wisdom from my Heavenly Father, the *perfect* Father:

> *For the LORD giveth wisdom: out of his mouth cometh knowledge and understanding.*—Proverbs 2:6

> *If any of you lack wisdom, let him ask of God, that giveth to all men liberally, and upbraideth not; and it shall be given him.* —James 1:5

> *Through wisdom is an house builded; and by understanding it is established.*—Proverbs 24:3

> *She openeth her mouth with wisdom; and in her tongue is the law of kindness.*—Proverbs 31:26

Last, she trusted God for the outcome. Jochebed did everything she could do, but ultimately she put Moses in the river and trusted God for the outcome. *We* know how the story turned out, but Jochebed had to trust God by faith.

We have to learn to "let go and let God." I love the illustration of the little boy whose hand was stuck in a very valuable vase. His parents tried everything they could to get his hand out, and nothing worked. After several hours of working to get his hand free, the vase had to be broken. As the vase broke into pieces, freeing his tiny hand, his parents saw for the first time that his fist was tightly clenched. As his little hand opened, everyone saw that he was clinging to a piece of candy! If only he would have let go of the candy, he could have easily taken his hand out of the vase. Perhaps you need to release your grip on the little things in life before God breaks your vase! Learn to trust Him!

How did it turn out for Jochebed? God gave Moses back to her *and* paid her to nurse and nurture him. God is so awesome! This type of outcome is the product of parental trust. Jochebed had to realize that God was in control, and she had to learn to trust Him, not knowing what the future would hold.

Training Children Consistently

Journal: Training children is not always easy, but today it paid off. I told Miriam to stand behind the bulrushes and watch her baby brother, and she did exactly what she was told. Praise the Lord.

"Consistency is the first of Christian duties." As much as we may agree with this statement, any parent knows that consistency is easier said than done—probably because the difficult assignment of being consistent is very time consuming. It only takes a minute to *tell* a child something, but it takes time and effort to *teach* the child the same thing effectively.

Consistently training our children to truly know the Lord should be our first priority in parenting. One of the saddest portions of Scripture to me is 1 Samuel 2:12 where it says, "*Now the sons of Eli were sons of Belial; they knew not the LORD.*" Hophni and Phinehas were sons of the priest, Eli, and they did not know the Lord. We must own our God-given responsibility as Christian parents to introduce our children to the Lord and to teach them to walk in His ways.

To know God, we must know His Word so we can educate our children in the Word of God, as well. The Bible is clear in Deuteronomy 6:6–9, "*And these words, which I command thee this day, shall be in thine heart: And thou shalt teach them diligently unto thy children, and shalt talk of them when thou sittest in thine house, and when thou walkest by the way, and when thou liest down, and when thou risest up. And thou shalt bind them for a sign upon thine hand, and they shall be as frontlets between thine eyes. And thou shalt write them upon the posts of thy house, and on thy gates."* Training through scriptural principles in a Christian home must take place 24/7. When it comes to instructing our children, we must first hide God's Word in our hearts so we can more easily impart His truth to them. We need to lead the way!

Dr. John Goetsch once shared these three simple ways to impart God's truth to others. Over the years, I have sought to apply these statements to my life as a parent.

Hide God's Word in our hearts. Children memorize much more easily than adults, so we should begin when they are young. The Bible says in 2 Timothy 3:15, *"And that from a child thou hast known the holy scriptures, which are able to make thee wise unto salvation through faith which is in Christ Jesus."*

Highlight God's Word in our homes. The government does not allow the Ten Commandments in public places, but we can still hang them in our homes! I encourage you to frame verses that are special to you and your family and place them in prominent places in your home. This is not only an inexpensive decorating idea; it also holds great spiritual value and eternal benefit.

Heed God's Word in our habits. After we have hidden God's Word in our hearts and highlighted His Word in our homes, we should heed His Word in our habits!

When it comes to establishing godly behavior in the home, be careful not to develop merely a list of rules. Eventually rules alone fall short for several reasons. First, the more rules you have, the more time you spend trying to remember which rule to enforce and what the penalty is. Second, it is impossible to make a rule for every conceivable scenario your children will face regarding temptation and sin. Third, the adult mind is not clever enough to make rules that the child's mind cannot somehow creatively circumvent!

So, we must consistently teach our children godly *principles.* We must equip them to respond to any given circumstance with godly character and according to Bible principles. I encourage you to begin teaching them virtues like these:

- Dependability
- Honesty
- Kindness
- Work Ethic
- Helpfulness
- Diligence
- Loyalty
- Faithfulness
- Righteousness
- Courage
- Stewardship
- Responsibility
- Contentment
- Self-control
- Moral Purity
- Love
- Conviction
- The Fear of the Lord

That should keep us busy for a while!

The first verse every husband quotes to his wife is Ephesians 5:22, *"Wives, submit...,"* and the first verse every mom teaches her child is Ephesians 6:1, *"Children, obey...."* And we all smile—right, ladies?! Seriously, "to obey your parents" is the one job that God specifically gives to children. It is *our* job then, to consistently teach our children to obey. We taught our children that delayed obedience is disobedience. That means we don't count—1, 2, 2 ¼, 2 ½, 2 ¾—you know the routine. They were to obey right away.

Our first year in Lancaster, my husband and I took our two children, Danielle and Larry, to Carl's Jr. for lunch as a treat. Danielle was four and Larry was two. We chose Carl's Jr. because it had an outside seating area with a little jungle gym filled with brightly colored balls. The kids could play while we enjoyed our lunch—it was a win-win situation. The patio was quite full that day, and the kids quickly ate their meals and went off to play in the balls.

As we watched the children at play, we noticed a big kid throwing the balls at all the others, and he was throwing them pretty hard! The children who were being hit began to call out for help after only a few moments. Pretty soon, this boy's mother intervened and told him to stop throwing the balls at other kids. Well, it was obvious that she had done a wonderful job training him, because he immediately continued to throw the balls, this time with even more force.

At this point, other moms started calling their children back to their tables. Upon seeing this, the boy's mother told him that they were leaving because he didn't obey. Again, the boy—knowing his mom had not reached her limit—continued to taunt the other children. Finally, the mother had enough. She stood up firmly and announced that they were leaving. The only problem was that her son did not move! So, she gave an ultimatum, "You come out now, or you're going to get it!" Still the boy did not obey. Then she said, "I will count to three, and you'd better be out of there!"

At this point, my husband thought we should leave, though I wanted to stay and see what would happen! By the time we called our children, gathered our things, and walked out of the play area, that poor woman was up to ten and still counting! She is what I would call a consistently *inconsistent* parent! She was training all right! She was training him that he could postpone obedience and get away with it. Her little boy knew that he had plenty of time before he really had to obey!

Earlier we looked at Deuteronomy 6:6–9, but God tells us in verse twenty four of that same chapter, *"And the LORD commanded us to do all these statutes, to fear the LORD our God, for our good always, that he might preserve us alive, as it is at this day."*

When you begin teaching obedience, be sure to define clearly what you are communicating. Children cannot obey if they don't know what you mean. We defined obedience to our children as "immediately doing what you are asked with a good heart attitude." We also established who they were to obey. They did not have to obey their brothers or sisters—and for this, they were glad. But they did have to obey Sunday school teachers, babysitters, or anyone who we placed in charge.

Don't get weary in well doing! Even when you are busy or tired, you should never overlook a direct disobedience. Many years ago, we went to a theme park in the San Francisco Bay area. It was similar to Sea World, but it also had a variety of jungle animal shows. We went to see the lion show and learned a great deal about parenting that day. We watched as each lion walked into a caged stage area and sat on its podium. The lion tamer stood in the middle of this area, surrounded by the lions. He went to one lion and commanded the lion to come off the podium, but the lion just sat there. In fact, the lion turned his head away from the tamer as if to say, "I can't see you; therefore, I can't hear you." (My children tried that one on me a few times when they were younger!) The tamer again told the lion to dismount, and again the lion did not obey. This went on for about twenty minutes. The people seated near us started complaining and shouting toward the stage. I thought there was going to be a riot, but eventually a voice came over the speaker and announced that we were free to leave, but the tamer could not let the lion disobey even one time. If it meant being there all day, the tamer had to win this battle of the wills. At that announcement, my husband looked at me and said, "If only parents were that diligent in training their children."

Remember to be specific in your requests to your children. For example, don't just say, "Go straighten up your room." "Straighten up your room" can mean a lot of different things—especially when children are involved! My idea of straightening up a room is vastly different from my children's ideas. Another example is "be quiet." What does that actually mean? Do I mean "be quieter than I am," "use your library voice," or "don't make a sound"? Be sure your child understands clearly what is expected when you make a request.

When it comes to discipline, be consistent as well. Explain the expectation, as well as the punishment. Say what you mean and mean what you say. Consistency eliminates confusion. A child who has consistent and loving discipline knows what to expect—which diffuses fear and increases understanding in the relationship.

Take Interest in the Good

Journal: I thank the Lord for this beautiful, healthy boy He has given me. I don't know all that God has in store for me or for him, but I know it is going to be something great.

Jochebed saw that Moses was a goodly child. Ask yourself, are you looking for the good in your child every day? Balance seems to be such a key word in my life. We balance the hot and cold water when we take a shower, we balance work and relaxation. Everyone tells us we need to have a balanced diet! We balance our tires, our checkbook...Yikes! I think I'll stop there. But do you balance praise with discipline? Are you taking interest in the good of your child?

Discipline is important to successful parenting, but so is encouragment and comfort. Read 1 Thessalonians 2:11, "*As ye know how we exhorted and comforted and charged every one of you, as a father doth his children.*"

It is far too easy to point out the negative in our children, without even intending to do so. Maybe you've heard the quote, "Some people find fault like there is a reward for it!" If you find yourself caught in the trap of seeing only the negative in your children, establish reminders to look for the good and recognize the victories. This area was a struggle for me at times, so I would often place 3 x 5 cards around the house that said, "Look for the good and praise it." This helped me remember to encourage and praise my children. I don't think we can truly understand the power of good, loving words nestled in the hearts of our children!

Here's a challenge: for every one negative interaction you have (and there will be plenty), make an effort to offset it with nine other positive interactions. For every one correction or lecture, make it your goal to say nine positive, encouraging, loving things to your child. The heart of a child cannot resist this kind of good communication. Be his cheerleader!

Not only should we use words to encourage and edify each other, but we should also avoid using certain words in our speech. It's important to speak respectfully to our children. Being the parent doesn't mean we have the right to speak harshly. Decide that there will be some words that are never to be said in your home. We taught our young children that there are some words such as "stupid," "shut up," or "loser" that are just as bad as curse words.

When Danielle was about three years old, we invited a recently saved family over for fellowship. This family had a little boy about Danielle's age. Everyone seemed to be having a great time, when suddenly the little boy came running into the dining room and said in front of God and everybody that Danielle had said a four-letter word! I was horrified. I stood up, grabbed Danielle by the hand and said, "Danielle, did you say a four-letter word?" With tears in her eyes she nodded and said, "Yes." I was embarrassed and upset, so I decided to take her upstairs. Halfway up the stairs my husband asked Danielle what she had said. I thought he was crazy—he was going to have her repeat it! With a trembling voice, she said she had called him "stupid"! Even though "stupid" was a bad word in our house, inside I was very relieved!

Again, here are some verses to commit to memory regarding our communication to each other at home:

> *Finally, brethren, whatsoever things are true, whatsoever things are honest, whatsoever things are just, whatsoever things are pure, whatsoever things are lovely, whatsoever things are of good report; if there be any virtue, and if there be any praise, think on these things.*—PHILIPPIANS 4:8

> *Let all bitterness, and wrath, and anger, and clamour, and evil speaking, be put away from you, with all malice: And be ye kind one to another, tenderhearted, forgiving one another, even as God for Christ's sake hath forgiven you.*—EPHESIANS 4:31–32

> *The words of a man's mouth are as deep waters, and the wellspring of wisdom as a flowing brook.*—PROVERBS 18:4

> *He that answereth a matter before he heareth it, it is folly and shame unto him.*—PROVERBS 18:13

> *Death and life are in the power of the tongue: and they that love it shall eat the fruit thereof.*—PROVERBS 18:21

As a side note, I strongly encourage you to read and study all of Proverbs 18. It's a powerful and helpful parenting chapter!

German writer, Johann Wolfgang von Goethe said, "If you treat a person as he is, he will stay as he is; but if you treat him as if he were what he ought to be and could be, he will become what he ought to be and could be." May we help our children reach their full potential for the Lord. We often think of potential only in terms of academic achievement, talent, or performance. Rather than pushing our children to be what *we* want them to be or expecting them to achieve what *we* desire, we should help them identify the strengths that God has given them and encourage them to be all *He* desires them to be.

Please don't misunderstand, I am not advocating lightening up on training, schoolwork, piano lessons, or important extracurricular activities (sorry kids!). All of this is vital in a child's development in the will of God. We must simply recognize that God has a plan for all of our children and that He has blessed them with unique gifts for unique purposes. Each child is a special creation of God, and it is easy to underestimate our children's potential in the will of God. We should endeavor to unlock that potential and develop it for the glory of God.

As parents, we may not be *solely* responsible for our children's reaching their potential, but we are pretty influential! We must instill in them a desire always to do their best for the Lord. Don't compare them to each other or to other families. Don't discourage their interests or neglect their gifts. Choose rather to fan the flames of good things in their lives. Look for the good constantly, and make a big deal out of little victories.

CHAPTER TEN

Developing Family Memories

ournal: By God's grace, and with all of us pitching in and doing our part, we did it! It wasn't always easy keeping such a little baby hidden, but I am so thankful we worked as a team. We are in this together.

Teamwork

The Bible says Jochebed hid Moses for three months. I am known for hiding things really well, but I cannot imagine hiding a baby for even one day!

Our youngest son, Matthew, received a puppy one year for Christmas. That same year, some friends allowed us to use their timeshare for a couple of days after Christmas, but we forgot that we had a new puppy to deal with! Of course, Matthew would have rather stayed home than leave his new dog, but the timeshare did not allow pets. After some thought, we made the ingenious decision to take the puppy with us and try to hide him for two days. He was so cute and so little, we figured no one would ever know! Wrong!

Within just a few hours of checking in, we were caught! Our little puppy, Krispy, had to go to a doggy hotel.

If hiding a puppy was that hard, I can't imagine hiding a baby for three months! (When my babies began to cry at night, I was sure that it woke up the entire neighborhood.) This had to be a tough task for Moses' family, and I'm sure that everyone had to do his part. They were a team.

Some years ago, the Lord impressed upon my husband's heart that our family should have a purpose or a mission statement. After much thought and prayer, we adopted the following as the purpose of our family: *"The mission of our family is to be a team that glorifies the Lord Jesus through obedience to His written Word and by edifying and exhorting one another as we grow to understand our diverse yet compatible personalities."*

In a team, everyone is needed and everyone is important. We each use our individual strengths toward a common goal. Some say it takes a village to raise a child. I think it takes a dad and a mom who are faithful to a good local church!

Not only do we need familial teamwork, we need the support of the local church. There is a cell phone commercial that I like. After buying a new cell phone, a man walks outside and suddenly he's surrounded by a group of technicians and customer service representatives. A bit surprised, he looks back at the sales clerk who says, "That's the support you get when you choose our cell phone service."

When I see that commercial, I can't help but be reminded of the amazing support that I have received, not only from my family, but also through the local church. I am so glad I have a loving church family, a youth pastor who encourages our goals, and school teachers who believe as we do. When one of us hurts, we all hurt. When one rejoices, we all rejoice. That's what teams are supposed to do! We are truly blessed.

Only let your conversation be as it becometh the gospel of Christ: that whether I come and see you, or else be absent, I may hear of your affairs, that ye stand fast in one spirit, with one mind striving together for the faith of the gospel.—PHILIPPIANS 1:27

Now I beseech you, brethren, by the name of our Lord Jesus Christ, that ye all speak the same thing, and that there be no divisions among you; but that ye be perfectly joined together in the same mind and in the same judgment.—1 CORINTHIANS 1:10

I therefore, the prisoner of the Lord, beseech you that ye walk worthy of the vocation wherewith ye are called, With all lowliness and meekness, with longsuffering, forbearing one another in love; Endeavouring to keep the unity of the Spirit in the bond of peace.—EPHESIANS 4:1–3

When it comes to developing family memories, teamwork is a pivotal starting point. Encourage teamwork at home and in the ministry. Endeavor to keep the unity of the Spirit in the bond of peace. Then enjoy the fruit of your labor as you create Christ-honoring memories with your family.

Treasure the Moment

Journal: This situation with baby Moses has reminded me that I don't know how long I have with each of my children. I must remember to cherish the time I do have with them. Before I know it, they will be grown—maybe even gone. I am thankful for the time I have with my family. I will always treasure the moment.

Life is too short. The Bible says it's a vapor! None of us know how long we will have together with our families. An o.b. nurse who was a friend of our family died within twenty-four hours of delivering her baby due to an infected needle. We have no guarantees for the future.

So enjoy every minute of being a mom! I'm thankful for caring mentors who counseled me to enjoy every stage of our children's lives. I remember all too well the many times I was ready to pull my hair out! But it was in those moments when someone would whisper in my ear, "Enjoy it, they'll be grown before you know it." With a slight smile and through gritted teeth, I politely tried to receive and heed their advice. You know what? They were right; it all passed so quickly.

Mom, don't be discouraged with the stage of parenting you are in right now! Your children will be grown before you know it, so enjoy *every* age of their lives. Though each life stage has its unique challenges, adjust your attitude to thinking, "This is the best age" or "I enjoy this phase the most." Seek to sincerely enjoy the moment.

Cherished family memories can come in many different ways, but they begin with a determination to treasure each moment. Purpose to start today!

Spend Time Together

I recently read a survey asking this question: "What makes your family great?" Among all the different answers, the most common was "the time we spend together."

Ladies often come to me complaining that they don't have enough family time. My answer to them is that there is only one *guarantee* to having family time: schedule it.

Scheduled Time. My husband and I go out to dinner together every so often, and we take our calendars for the purpose of scheduling future date nights and special family time. Not all of these scheduled family times are extravagant. The true focus is simply being together. Yet we have found if we don't schedule it, then it just won't happen.

For a while, our kids had the idea that family time meant doing something big like going to Disneyland or going out to a special restaurant. They would often ask, "Is today a family day?" or, "Can we have a family night tonight?" I encouraged them to change their perspective and to realize that *every* time we are together is special—no matter what we are doing!

Our family time varies widely. Sometimes it is planned by my husband. Other times I will put together a plan. We even allow the kids to pick a family activity from time to time. Our best family nights usually happen right at home. With a little imagination and not much expense, these special nights can provide great fun and cherished memories for years to come.

Spontaneous Time. Looking back over the years, I believe our favorite family times have been spontaneous! Isn't it funny how the unplanned events are usually the ones we enjoy the most?

Recently, our family was driving home from a meeting in Los Angeles. Out of nowhere, my husband asked our daughter Kristine, to call Staples Center to see if the Lakers were playing that night. To our surprise and delight, they were! So on the spur of the moment, my husband took the whole family to the Lakers' game. It was a time we will never forget! The look on their faces that night reminded me of the word used in the popular MasterCard commercial—priceless!

You can't develop family memories if you're not spending time together! Evaluate your schedule, allow some spontaneous activity every now and then, and delight in the simple joy of being together!

Keep a Right Spirit during Interruptions

Interruptions are an inevitable aspect of ministry life. Unfortunately, sometimes an emergency will arise and family time has to be rescheduled. Don't let this rob your joy or dampen your spirit. Instead, schedule plenty of family time far enough in advance, and then be flexible as the Lord leads.

Mom, keep in mind that if a crisis takes place and you have to reschedule family time, the kids will be watching your reaction.

If you whine and complain, they could become bitter and resentful toward the ministry.

Several years ago, we had a big family vacation planned. It was going to be the first time for us to fly together as a family. Two days before we left, a dear senior saint in our church passed away, and my husband had promised her months before that he would do her memorial service. Our bags were packed, our tickets were ready, and we had a dilemma.

My husband and I decided that the kids and I would travel ahead of him, and he would fly to join us the next day. As you can imagine, this was a very difficult decision for both of us, but rather than grumble or complain, I resolved to make this experience fun and adventurous for those of us traveling without dad.

Time and space do not permit me to share the incredible chain of events that unfolded on that portion of our vacation. The things that happened between the time we were dropped off at the airport and the time he joined us the next day were absolutely comical. Every time we remember that vacation, the kids and I can't stop laughing about it. It all turned out just fine, and we had another set of great memories to cherish. God gave us a wonderful vacation that year and honored our decision to have a right spirit when things weren't seemingly "going our way."

Now think about that. What pastor's wife and kids don't want dad completely free of ministry obligations during family vacation? It's the one time a year that we get him all to ourselves, right? It would have been so easy to have whined, pitched a fit, and said some pretty negative (but true) remarks. And the result of our displeasure would have been six miserable people, bad memories, and potentially four children who resented dad, God, and the ministry!

I had a magnet once that said, "If Mama ain't happy, ain't nobody happy." Remember that the next time the unexpected happens. Keep your spirit right and your heart sweet, and watch to see how God will intervene on your behalf.

Take Trips Together

Schedule trips together as a family. Everybody occasionally needs a break from the routine. These breaks can be anything from a day-trip to a full-blown family vacation. The duration of the vacation isn't the point! Time together is!

I believe it is vital for our children to have times when they get their dad and mom all to themselves. This won't happen if you don't make it a priority. Plan it, budget it, and enjoy it.

Some pastors feel guilty for taking this kind of time off. They worry about what people will think or about what isn't getting done while they are away. They feel the pressure to model a strong work ethic (which is needful) and to meet the constant demands of a growing ministry.

Years ago, we decided that these times were not only healthy for *our* family, but they were healthy for the *church family* as well. This is true for a number of reasons.

First, the church will always be strengthened when the pastor and his family are strengthened. A pastor with a balanced, healthy family will always be a better leader and preacher.

Second, the church family will often emulate in their own families what they see modeled. What better example can a pastor set than when he is spending time with his family, loving his wife, and nurturing his children? Let your church know that your family spends time together, and encourage them to do the same.

During the twenty years that we have served the Lord at Lancaster Baptist, we have taken regular family vacations every year. Now that our kids are nearly grown, we treasure every one of them. In addition to this, we've made regular retreats (as a couple and as a family) a part of our annual calendar. Every trip has served to make us a stronger family and more effective servants of Christ.

Develop Family Traditions

Family traditions have been very helpful in creating family memories at the Chappell home. These fun times create a sense of unity and belonging and they bring the family together in a unique way.

We have a lot of traditions. Some are deep rooted and enduring. For example, we always read Luke 2 on Christmas morning before we open presents. Another example is our traditional stop at the Cracker Barrel Restaurant in Flagstaff, Arizona, whenever we are returning from the family farm in Colorado.

For years, my husband drove our kids to school in the mornings, and they had a little tradition in the car. They all tried to be the first person to say, "It sure is a beautiful day!" Then they usually ended up singing some silly song along the way. I think the song made them glad that we only live a mile away, but it was tradition nonetheless.

Some traditions have a shorter life span. For a long time we had hamburgers every Saturday night as a family. But, eventually that got old, and we switched the menu. When the kids were little we had a "child of the week." The child of the week sat in the front seat, picked his favorite breakfast cereal from the store, and went first when we played a game. That worked until the kids got older and had their own cars. Danielle, Larry, and Kristine now say that Matthew is spoiled—he's child of the *year* (and that's just fine with him)!

Some traditions flop right out of the gate and quickly become non-traditions—like when we slept out in our backyard in a tent. That was one we'll never forget! But for some reason, no one wanted to do it again. Don't be afraid to try something adventurous as a family, even if the final consensus is "let's not make that a tradition!"

Make Memories by Talking

Finally, we make memories by talking, and one of *our* favorite places to talk is at the dinner table. We have always tried to make dinnertime a happy time, not a time to discuss detentions or negative things. My husband eats pretty fast and typically finishes his meal before the rest of us are even half through. So he usually begins the conversation by saying "Let's tell a…" He ends the statement with "favorite dinner," "best vacation," "most embarrassing moment," and so on. Each person at the table takes a turn sharing answers. We laugh. We cry. We savor the memories. We love it!

Another good time for talking is at bedtime. What kid wouldn't rather talk than sleep? When the children were little we used to go to their rooms and tuck them in. Of course, they would always want a story. As they got a little older, we would sit on their beds and just talk. Sometimes the talks were short, other times they were long. Now that *they* are older, we have a new tradition. They come to *our* room and say goodnight to *us*. They all gather around our small queen-size bed and talk for sometimes hours! It doesn't get any better than that.

This chapter may have seemed to apply more to family life than to ministry, but in my opinion, it all goes together. Our family is our first ministry, and we serve God together as a family.

Making family memories is a way to draw the hearts of your family together and to the Lord. These memories will fill your heart and your children's hearts for years to come. Make their experiences in ministry, in church, and at home positive and worth remembering. Nurture their hearts toward the Lord and His will by planning and providing time to laugh and play together.

Make memories. Video them. Photograph them. Put them into scrapbooks and photo albums. Look at them often. Some of our best family nights take place when we pull out old family photos or videos, and simply spend the night reminiscing!

I read the following quote recently: "My grandmother made me a scrapbook because I was once too young to remember; I am making scrapbooks for my family because one day I may be too old to remember." Preserve the memories for your children *and* for yourself! You will be glad you did!

CHAPTER ELEVEN

Praying for Your Husband

She will do him good and not evil all the days of her life.
—PROVERBS 31:12

Reasons To Pray

A bride was very nervous just moments before her wedding—so nervous that she wasn't sure she could even walk down the aisle. Her mother decided to give her some words of calming wisdom. She said to her, "Honey, there are only three things you need to focus on. If you think about these three things, you'll be fine.

"The first is walking down the aisle. Just focus on walking down the aisle of the church. I know it's rather long, but just concentrate on that. Don't get caught up with those on either side of the aisle. Just focus on getting to the end of the aisle.

"Next, focus on the altar. It is your destination today. Make your way down the aisle to the altar. There you will stand before

God with the man you love and will make vows to God and him. He will also make vows to you. Focus on the altar that represents the love God has for you in Jesus Christ.

"Lastly, focus on the hymn that the soloist will sing. In poetry and song, the hymn embodies God's love for you in Christ, your love for your husband, and his love for you. So to help you not be so nervous, focus on those three things—walking down the aisle, standing before the altar, and listening to the hymn."

The bride was very thankful to her mom for her words of advice. The gathering of family and friends watched as she walked down the aisle and noticed a look of calm determination on her face. But as she passed them, they began to chuckle quietly. For along with the look of calm determination, she was mumbling three words over and over to help calm her nerves. As she passed them, they heard her saying, "Aisle, Altar, Hymn…Aisle, Altar, Hymn…Aisle, Altar, Hymn…."

Many women enter marriage with this underlying determination—"I'll alter him" (even though they may protest that their intentions are to change him for his own good). Well, *my* intention in this chapter is not to give you ways to change your husband, but to show you a way to change *yourself*!

If you are hurting in your marriage right now, your first emotional response to the advice in this chapter may be anger. You may be tempted to respond by shifting the blame or excusing your own attitude: "What about me?", "But, he doesn't…", "Why do I have to do…?" Be willing and open to change areas in your life as God reveals the need.

Too often I see couples dig in their heels against each other, refusing to give in. They withhold what the other spouse needs or wants in a determined effort to get their own way. But it's never right to refuse to do what is right! As you read these words, may you be encouraged to surrender—to lay down your arms and quit fighting—regardless of what your spouse does. Whether your marriage is struggling or soaring, examine *your* role, and not only the needs of your husband. Decide that, with God's help, you will be the best *wife* you can be!

I believe the greatest way I can lift up the heart of my husband is by praying for him. Hudson Taylor said, "It is possible to move men, through God, by prayer alone." We must realize that we are not our husbands' "change agent." God is. If our husbands need to change in an area, only God can truly bring about that transformation.

If you are struggling in your marriage, then take one hundred percent of your energy and focus on doing something positive for your husband. The most important and the most positive thing you can do for him is to pray for him!

Prayer is one of the greatest unclaimed resources I have as a wife and as a Christian. Psalm 121:1–2 says, *"I will lift up mine eyes unto the hills, from whence cometh my help. My help cometh from the LORD, which made heaven and earth."* Each wife brings different gifts to her husband's ministry, but the one gift that every wife can offer is that of covering her husband in prayer. No one knows your husband like you know him. There is no one else who can completely relate to him and what he is facing like you can. Therefore, no one can pray for him like you can pray for him!

Prayer Increases Faith

Dr. Howard Hendricks, a Christian educator, was asked how to teach children to have faith. His answer: instruct them to keep a prayer list! Truly, prayer increases faith.

God often answered prayer in mighty ways during my early married life. It was during those times that my faith increased greatly. Right after our oldest son, Larry, was born, finances became very tight. We didn't have any food in the house and my husband was going with our pastor and other staff members to a pastor's conference. The devil kept telling me what a great time my husband was going to have. I imagined that he would be going out to restaurants, eating, and laughing with all the other pastors while I would be home alone with the two kids and nothing to eat.

My husband didn't even seem to notice or care. One Sunday afternoon, I couldn't hold it in any longer. I told my husband how I felt about his leaving us with no money and no food. I went so far as to say, "Fine, I'll go stay with my parents. They'll take care of us!" That was probably the worst thing I ever said to my husband!

He didn't even retaliate. He simply said, "Let's pray," and immediately he got down on his knees and started to pray. To my shame, I was not in the mood to pray, so I just stood there. As he began praying, the phone rang. I decided to answer it, since I wasn't praying anyway. There was a preacher on the phone. He said that *he* was just praying, and God brought to his memory that my husband had preached for him a few months back, and he never gave him a love offering. He wanted to bring the check over to our house right then. That preacher was Brother Wally Davis, a dear friend who has since gone home to be with the Lord. God answered prayer that day, and I asked my husband and God to forgive me. My faith had just increased, and I had learned a valuable lesson.

Another growing moment took place shortly after moving to Lancaster. My husband was shaking hands at the door one Sunday evening when one of our families invited our family to join them at a local fast food restaurant called Naugles. This invitation was a real blessing, because we were low on food and money at the time. Being treated to tacos for dinner would have truly been an answer to prayer!

After my husband finished locking up the building, we headed to Naugles. On the way there, he informed me that these families would probably already be eating and that we would need to pay for our own dinner. That wasn't a good thing, because we simply didn't have any money! We had come to Lancaster by faith, and at that particular moment, we had nothing *but* faith!

When I told him I didn't have any money, he didn't believe me! He asked me to check my purse again, and he even had

Danielle and Larry checking the seat cushions of the car for any spare change. After a few moments, we had managed to find about seventy-six cents—barely enough to buy a small drink. So, we told the kids that we were going to buy one drink to share and informed them that they were not allowed to say that they were hungry!

It was hard going to a restaurant hungry, knowing you couldn't eat and knowing there wasn't any food at home either. But, this was our new church family, and we wanted desperately to fellowship and develop meaningful relationships with them. We walked into Naugles and headed to the counter to get our small drink, when the lady at the counter held out two huge bags of food and said to my husband, "You are not going to believe what just happened! A van load of teenagers came through the drive-thru and ordered all this food. When they got to the window, they just sped off. Now we have all this food that will go to waste…would you like to have it?" My husband and I just stood there and cried.

Ironically, the only thing that group of teenagers did *not* order was a drink, so we ordered a small iced tea. We ate that night until we could not eat another bite. We even had enough food left over for the next morning, but the story doesn't end there.

Brother Rick and Kathy Houk, who served at a church three hours away, arrived at our house that next morning with a station-wagon filled with groceries. Brother Houk took an offering for our family the night before in their church service, and God led him to buy groceries and drive through the night to bring us food that morning. God is so good, and once again He provided for the needs of our family! Needless to say, faith had increased!

When we first moved to Lancaster, we saw God answer so many of our prayers, but after a while, I began to doubt that God was actually answering *my* prayers. I figured He was really answering my husband's prayers, since we prayed about the same things. I desperately needed to see God answer my prayers personally. So I had a prayer request that I did not share with

anyone—not even my husband. I wanted to know for sure that
God was interested in answering my seemingly insignificant
prayers.

It was getting close to September, and Danielle was going to
be starting Kindergarten. I would be home-schooling her, which
for me was great. I was happy to keep her home for one more
year! At the same time, I was a little sad for Danielle that she
wasn't going to experience that first day of school like I thought
she would—no line to stand in, no lunch box to carry, no one to
trade her snacks with, no desk to put her books in.

That's when I decided I was going to pray that God would
provide Danielle a desk for her very first day of school. I
envisioned putting her name on it and making a big deal of it so
that she would remember her first day of school.

We didn't have any money, so I knew that God would have
to supply it. I began to pray every day for a desk for Danielle and
told no one but the Lord. At first, I was excited to see how God
was going to answer this prayer. But when days and weeks passed
and we still had no desk, I began to doubt the Lord. I thought,
"See, God doesn't want to answer my prayers!"

It was Labor Day, the day before we were going to start
school, and still, there was no desk. So, I decided that at this
point, God needed my help! I thought my husband and I could
go shopping and look for the desk that I was sure God wanted us
to have. But my plans were not working! Early that morning, a
church family invited us to spend Labor Day with them going to
deserted gold mines in the middle of the Mojave Desert! Yippee!

My first thought was "Where am I going to find a desk in the
middle of a deserted gold mine?" I couldn't tell my husband about
my plans because I didn't want him to know about my prayer
request.

So we went to the Mojave Desert. I have to admit I wasn't
very talkative. I was too intent on looking for a desk on the side
of the road! Once, we passed an old junk yard. I made a big deal

about how I wanted to go through the old junk yard. I couldn't tell them why. I'm sure my husband thought his wife was losing it. I normally didn't act this way. But I didn't want God to fail! (Isn't it silly how we rationalize things?)

As we stopped the van to look through the junkyard, I just knew there was going to be a desk there, but there wasn't even anything I could make *look* like a desk. I was pretty quiet the rest of the day. When we got home, I went straight to bed, thinking that God didn't care about me, Danielle, or our family when we were just trying to serve Him.

I couldn't sleep. I just lay there rehearsing all that took place that day. Then, I heard the phone ring and my husband answered it. I heard him say, "Just a minute, I'll ask Terrie." He yelled out, "Terrie, would you like a desk for Danielle? We can get it tonight."

Remember my husband still did not have a clue about my prayer—in fact, no one did! I jumped out of bed so fast and with such glee that I'm sure my husband was convinced I had gone over the edge. Some members of our church came right over with a school desk that they no longer needed, and moments later I was putting Danielle's nametag on it!

The next morning, on her first day of school, she had her very own desk. Yet I was the one who learned one of the greatest lessons of my life that day. God does answer my prayers, and God does care about His children. He may not answer the way we want Him to or in the time frame that we think He should. But, He *is* able to do exceedingly more than we ask or think. That day my faith increased tremendously. Now, twenty years later, God is still providing and my faith continues to grow every day.

Prayer Releases Burdens

Prayer also allows us to release our burdens. All of us carry burdens whether we talk about them or not, and prayer gives us the opportunity to unload our cares on the Lord. It is so much better to go to the Lord instead of unloading on our husbands or, worse yet, another woman! God doesn't repeat what I tell Him, He does not judge what I say, and He understands everything. Ladies sometimes come to me for counsel, and the first thing they say to me is, "You just don't understand." I tell them they're probably right, but I know Someone who does. The Bible says in Psalm 147:5, "*Great is our Lord, and of great power: his understanding is infinite.*" I love this verse. Not only does the Lord understand, but He has the power to do something about the burden!

Go get yourself a glass of water. How heavy is a glass of water? You may answer that it depends on whether it is one cup or two cups. But, that doesn't matter. What matters is how long you hold it. If you hold the glass for just a minute, it would not be heavy at all. But what if you held it for an hour or two hours? Your arms would probably start crying out in pain. What if you held it for a day? You would probably have to get medical attention. The weight of the cup of water doesn't change, but the longer you hold it, the heavier it feels and the more damage it can do to you.

The longer we hold onto our burdens, the heavier they become to our heart. God never intended for us to carry our life's burdens alone. First Peter 5:7 says, "*Casting all your care upon him; for he careth for you.*" God wants to bear our load. He designed us to need His help in carrying the weight that life puts on our shoulders.

John Baillie said, "Give me a stout heart to bear my own burdens. Give me a willing heart to bear the burdens of others. Give me a believing heart to cast all burdens upon Thee, O Lord."

What burdens are you carrying today? Are you tired of hauling them around? Are they becoming heavier and heavier to your heart? Friend, I encourage you to cast your cares upon Him. You weren't meant to bear your burdens alone, and God is eager to carry your load. He is waiting to hear from you.

Prayer Reminds Us of God's Nearness

Prayer teaches us that God is always near. We are the ones who shy away from God. It's not the other way around! Hebrews 10:22

tells us, *"Let us draw near with a true heart in full assurance of faith, having our hearts sprinkled from an evil conscience, and our bodies washed with pure water."*

Oswald Chambers said, "The purpose of prayer is to reveal the presence of God equally present all the time in every condition." And Psalm 145:18 promises, *"The LORD is nigh unto all them that call upon him, to all that call upon him in truth."*

When Danielle was about three years old, we took a family vacation with my husband's family. My mother-in-law and I decided to take the kids to the pool and let them splash around for a while.

A few moments later, Danielle was in one of those inflatable turtles at the shallow end of the pool, and we were sitting on the edge of the pool with our legs in the water. Danielle was just inches from us. We were somewhat lost in conversation when I suddenly realized that she had fallen under the turtle and was standing perfectly still beneath the water, looking up at me. I reached down and immediately pulled her out. It was a startling moment for all of us.

The strange thing is, she could have easily reached out to me. I was sitting very close to her and able to help! But for some reason, Danielle did not move in the water.

This story reminds me of so many Christian ladies today. Often, we feel like we are drowning under the burdens and pressures of life, when all we have to do is reach out to the Lord. He is close by, waiting to help, ready to strengthen us, yet we just stand there alone.

The question is not, "How close is God?" The question is, "Will you reach out to Him?" He is as near to you as He has always been. Why not reach out to Him right now, seek His help, and cast yourself upon Him in full and complete dependence?

Prayer Provides Power

There is power in prayer—not because of what we pray, but because God is powerful. Edwin Harvey said, "A day without prayer is a day without blessing, and a life without prayer is a life without power." God has the power to transform you, your circumstances, your husband, and your marriage. On the other hand, Satan wants to destroy your marriage and the only way you can truly defeat him is through prayer!

> No one is a firmer believer in the power of prayer than the devil; not that he practices it, but he suffers from it.
> —Guy H. King

A tale is told about a small town that had been historically "dry," but a local businessman decided to build a tavern. A group of Christians from the town church were concerned and planned an all-night prayer meeting to ask God to intervene. It just so happened that shortly thereafter, lightning struck the bar and it burned to the ground.

The owner of the bar sued the church, claiming that the prayers of the congregation were responsible. The church hired a lawyer to argue in court that they were not to blame.

The presiding judge, after his initial review of the case, stated, "No matter how this case is decided, one thing is clear. The tavern owner believes in the power of prayer and the Christians do not." I think this tale is a sad but true commentary on the lives of many Christians today.

Don't settle for a life lived in your own strength and effort. Ask God for His power, depend on it for a fruitful Christian life, and give Him the glory as He works on your behalf.

> *Confess your faults one to another, and pray one for another, that ye may be healed. The effectual fervent prayer of a righteous man availeth much.*—James 5:16

Prayer Changes Our Lives

Prayer changes us! That truth gives us another reason for coming before the throne of God.

I saw a sign in a gift shop that read, "Prayer changes things." I have found that prayer doesn't necessarily always change "things," but it does always change me.

Usually, our perspective in prayer is not that *we* need to change, but *something* or *someone* else needs to change. I read this statement recently, and it made me laugh. "A man marries a woman hoping she'll never change. A woman marries a man hoping he'll change. And, they're both disappointed." Sometimes our prayers are focused more on altering someone else than on allowing the Holy Spirit to transform us! Don't try to conform your husband into your image, but rather pray that he would be conformed into the image of Jesus Christ.

Each day, I pray that my husband will get a new wife—me—a more Christ-like me! Our prayer should always be, "Lord, *I* am standing in the need of prayer…change *me*."

I genuinely hope that these "reasons" to pray have challenged you to have a right perspective in your marriage—a prayer perspective! May your sincere desire be to bring your heart to God consistently in prayer for your husband.

As we serve the Lord with our husbands, prayer will keep our hearts tender, our lives growing, and our relationship with the Lord and with our husbands strong. Please allow me to share some things that have been helpful in developing my heart for prayer and for my husband.

Praying for Myself

Nothing can make the difference in our marriages more than prayer can make. As stated earlier, when I go to the Lord in prayer, I pray for myself first. I want there to be nothing between my soul and my Saviour. Psalm 66:18 warns, *"If I regard iniquity in my heart, the Lord will not hear me."* Make this psalm a prayer of your heart, *"Examine me, O LORD, and prove me; try my reins and my heart"* (Psalm 26:2).

My husband carries many burdens, and I decided a long time ago that I don't want to be one of them! I don't want to be his burden; I want to be his helpmeet. I desire to lighten his load, not increase it. Perhaps the greatest way to uplift the heart of my husband is by staying spiritually strong as I serve with him. I want him to know that he doesn't have to worry about my spiritual wellbeing.

I use the following acrostic to help me pray effectively:

P —Praise. Praise the Lord for His attributes and thank Him for His goodness.
R —Repent. Confess all known sin. Keep short accounts with God.
A —Ask. Take requests to God.
Y —Yield. Yield to the Lord and to His Word.
E —Everyone. Then pray for others: family, missionaries, pastors' wives, friends.
R —Read God's Word. Conclude your time of prayer by listening to God through His Word.

Another acrostic that works well as a prayer pattern is ACTS:

A —Adoration
C —Confession
T —Thanksgiving
S —Supplication

My prayer is that I would fulfill the roles that God has given me and in the way that would be pleasing to Him! I have listed some areas that are on my personal prayer list in hopes that it may be a help to you. There are enough that I could pray specifically for one each day for a month. Here is what I pray...

- That I will be the Christian God wants me to be
- That I would be Spirit-filled all the time
- That I will be a good wife for my husband
- That I will be the right mother for our four children
- That I would live holy
- That I would be a good example as a church member

- That I would be soul-conscious
- That I will be a Christ-like teacher
- That I would be a good steward with my time, talent, and treasures
- That I would be a thoughtful daughter and daughter-in-law
- That I will be a fine citizen
- That I will possess a servant's heart
- That I will not be selfish
- That I will be compassionate
- That I will have a good attitude
- That I won't be insensitive to the needs of my husband
- That I would be as forgiving as the Lord is to me
- That I won't be easily offended
- That I would be my husband's recreational partner
- That I would be joyful
- That I would show my husband that he is respected
- That I would be kind
- That I would be frugal
- That I would not be a nagging wife
- That I would manage the house in a way that is pleasing to my husband
- That I would prepare healthy and tasty meals
- That I would be a good listener
- That I would be thankful for the little things
- That I would edify my husband
- That I would be patient
- That I would avoid every appearance of evil
- That I would honor my husband
- That I would not hold any bitterness in my heart

Praying for My Husband

Look not every man on his own things, but every man also on the things of others.—Philippians 2:4

Praying for my husband allows me to have a positive impact in his life. Something usually happens when we pray for others, especially for our husbands. When we pray for our husbands, the hardness in our heart softens, our anger recedes, our hurts are healed, and forgiveness takes place. I have a picture of my husband as a little boy that I keep with my prayer journal. It reminds me that my husband is one of God's children, and I ask God to help me see my husband through His eyes. After this kind of prayer and after looking at that picture, I find it very hard to be upset with him.

You can pray for your husband in a variety of ways. How you pray for him, however, is not as important as consistently and frequently lifting Him up before the Lord.

Pray for your husband's specific needs. The following list may help as you develop a greater and more detailed prayer life for your husband. Pray:

- That he will be Spirit filled
- That he will have a strong walk with the Lord
- That he will have a productive day
- That God will bless his appointments
- That he will be able to handle the stress of the day
- That God will give him wisdom in counseling
- That he would have a sense of fulfillment
- That he would have sufficient study time
- That God will strengthen him in his burdens
- That God will protect him from temptation
- That God will give protection from anyone wanting to hurt him
- That God will protect his reputation
- That he will be healthy—keep him well
- That God will heal him if he is sick
- For his responsibilities
- For his priorities
- That he will be a good leader
- For those that he leads
- For his role as a father
- For safety as he travels
- For refreshment as he travels
- For no delays as he travels
- That God will make him strong where he is weak
- That God will give him the courage to make right choices

- That he will be encouraged
- For his vision
- That God will direct his path
- That he will be fruitful
- For his friends
- For safety from any danger
- That he would maintain balance in all his roles
- For sermons he is preparing
- That God will safeguard his heart
- That he will continue to love righteousness and hate wickedness
- That he will have self-control
- That he will have peace and joy
- That God will give him wisdom in disciplining the children
- That he will recognize the lies of the enemy

This list is not exhaustive, but it gives us a starting point! These are things for which we can pray every day. Imagine the profound impact you could have on your husband's life and ministry if you would bring these requests before the Lord on a regular basis. Imagine how your heart might fill with a deeper love for God and for him!

You can also pray for your husband from head to toe as Sylvia Gunter recommends in her book, *Prayer Portions*.

His head—That he may lead you
His mind—That he may know Christ
His eyes—That he may see from God's perspective and be aware of spiritual danger
His ears—That he may hear God's words with his heart
His nose—That he will be a refreshing fragrance
His mouth—That he would have boldness in speaking of Christ and wisdom to keep the door of his lips
His bones—That he would be healthy
His heart—That he would obey with his whole heart
His arms—That God would be his arm every morning—Isaiah 33:2
His hands—That he will bless God as long as he lives—Psalm 63:4
His legs—That he will walk by faith
His feet—That God will direct his steps[4]

Another aspect of my prayer time is thankfulness. Let me encourage you not to take for granted the good qualities your husband possesses. Be thankful to the Lord for the way your husband provides and for the person he is. (By the way, it wouldn't hurt to thank your husband too!)

Somewhere along life's journey, I noticed that I forgot to be thankful for all the little things my husband does for me. So, I now purpose to spend time every day thanking the Lord for my husband's positive attributes. I thank the Lord that he:

- Trusts God
- Leads our home in spiritual matters
- Takes a stand for what is right
- Fixes things that are broken at the house (or has a professional do it)
- Is faithful to me
- Preaches the Word of God without compromise
- Spends time with the children
- Provides us with a nice home
- Plans family time
- Keeps the Lord first
- Is honest
- Is forgiving
- Works hard
- Finishes a project
- Lives by principle
- Follows the Scriptures
- Writes notes to the kids often
- Puts gas in my car
- Leads in family devotions
- Stays strong spiritually
- Gives me foot massages after we host a group of people in our home
- Checks for noises in the middle of the night
- Tells me that he loves me
- Sometimes sits with me in church (That's not very often for a pastor's wife!)

- Asks for my opinion
- Tries to remember my favorite kind of chocolate
- Calls to say he is going to be late
- Never goes to bed angry
- Keeps growing as a Christian
- Is my best friend
- Makes our marriage a priority

Pray with Our Husbands

Not only do I pray for myself and for my husband, I also like to pray *with* my husband. This takes some determination and even some planning, but the results are worth it. Together, we can share burdens and blessings, and together, we can be assured that we are right with each other and right with God.

It is impossible to come before the Lord when you are angry with your husband, and determining to pray together will be a powerful step in resolving struggles and coming together as one in the Lord. Matthew 18:20 gives us this promise: *"For where two or three are gathered together in my name, there am I in the midst of them."*

The adage, "A family that prays together stays together," certainly is true! When my husband and I pray together we not only pray for each other, but we also pray for our children and their specific needs. We also pray for our finances, our offerings, and our ministry. We bring our goals before the Lord. We pray that our marriage will draw us closer to the Lord and closer to each other. We pray that we will be a team, united in spirit and in commitment to each other. Then we pray for others for whom we are burdened.

The most important thing we can do each day is to spend time in prayer. God tells us to pray without ceasing. It is a command that we should not take flippantly. At the end of the day, prayer is our best defense for our marriage, and it's the best way to uplift the heart of your husband.

When we go to the family farm in southwest Colorado, my husband always takes me to what he affectionately calls "the point." It is a canyon rim on the border of our extended family's property. He likes to do some target practice there and always wants me to shoot the gun. I don't feel comfortable holding a gun, and I don't know if I could actually shoot it "for real"—but for some odd reason he wants me to be "armed and dangerous"!

When we go to the Lord in prayer, we become "armed and dangerous" against Satan, and he knows it. "The devil trembles when he sees the weakest Christian on his knees." Always remember that prayer succeeds when all else fails.

May God give you the grace to begin walking with Him in prayer every day. May you pray consistently for your husband, and may your marriage reap the many benefits that prayer will bring. God is interested in *your* prayers, not just your husband's! Whether you're praying for a school desk, tomorrow's food, or some other need, He is always near, He is always listening, and He will respond to your faith.

Something tells me that the virtuous woman of Proverbs was a lady who prayed for her husband—for the heart of her husband was safely trusting in her! May God give you grace to be that kind of wife for your husband.

CHAPTER TWELVE

Lifting Up the Heart of Your Husband: Part One

retired couple was at home one day when the husband stated that he was going out for an hour. "While you're out, could you pick up some trash bags and a gallon of milk?" asked his wife. "No problem," he said. "Now, write it down so you won't forget." "I won't forget," said the husband, "It's in here (pointing to his head), and it won't get out." To which the wife replied, "Now dear, you have the habit of forgetting things. You'd better write it down." "I don't need to write it down. I won't forget," he insisted.

About an hour later the husband returned and plopped two turkey sub sandwiches down on the table.

The wife looked at the two subs, sighed, and said to her husband, "I told you that you would need to write things down. You forgot the sodas!"

In today's culture, our calendars are filled to capacity with events and activities. We are busier than we ever have been, and in the midst of all our busyness, we forget the most basic and important things in our lives.

Have you forgotten that you are your husband's helpmeet? You were created to be his helper! You exist to help him fulfill his holy calling and reach his full potential. Are you living out your God-given purpose?

Encouraging your husband or living your life as a helpmeet does not mean that you become so absorbed in your husband that you have no individual value or that you lose your unique identity in Christ. It does not mean that you become a "doormat" with no valuable ideas, input, or opinions. It's not about forfeiting your influence or simply becoming an appeasing woman. It's also not about becoming a quiet manipulator, and attempting to get your own way through more subtle avenues. It's not about reshaping your husband to fulfill your own dreams or desires.

These three traps—absorption, appeasement, and manipulation—are actually subtle forms of control. Uplifting your husband's heart is not about controlling him. It's about encouraging him to let God control him. It's about supporting the work of God in his heart and the will of God for his life.

This chapter does not contain any new or secret principles. In fact, you may already know the importance of each of them, but perhaps you have become slack in fulfilling your primary role as a wife. Maybe you have failed to make your responsibility as an encourager your first priority. In the last chapter we saw the first way we can lift the heart of our husband is by prayer, but there are other ways that God will use you to encourage and strengthen your husband. Let's find out more!

Protect Him

The devil wants to devastate your home and destroy your ministry. He's out to ruin all of us, so I recommend that we become proactive in resisting his tactics. Let's not just stand by and watch!

First Peter 5:8 says, *"Be sober, be vigilant; because your adversary the devil, as a roaring lion, walketh about, seeking whom he may devour:"* I refuse to live passively while the devil has his way with my home or ministry.

God has given me an area of responsibility. He has given me a husband whom I should watch over in the way that the Lord would have me to. Now, I don't mean that it is my job to protect him in the same sense that he protects me! I am 5' 2" and weigh too many pounds, but I still couldn't physically protect him from even a spider! I realize there are many areas where I am incapable of protecting my husband. I do believe, however, there are a few aspects of life in which God *wants* me to be his protector.

I believe the key to protecting your husband is spiritual alertness. Proverbs 31:27 says, *"She looketh well to the ways of her household, and eateth not the bread of idleness."*

I have been known to be oblivious to what is happening right in front of me. Not too long ago, my husband took me to get something cold to drink. As we were walking out the door of the restaurant, another man was coming in and he opened the door for us. I said, "Thank you" and kept on walking. A few steps later I noticed that my husband was not with me. He was still talking to the man at the door. So I waited there in the parking lot drinking my Diet Coke, oblivious to what was happening nearby.

A moment later, another gentleman ran up to me in a panic and said, "Did you just see that accident?" My response was, "What accident?" Less than thirty feet away from where I was standing, a car had just been rear ended and had crashed into a light pole! I didn't see or hear a thing! (This is why I pray that God will keep me alert!)

I pray that I will be observant of any danger lurking in the shadows of our relationship or ministry. I want to be aware of any woman who seems to crave the attention of my husband. He has made this job easy for me by establishing boundaries. Nearly all of his counseling is with men or with couples. He will not counsel a lady unless I am present or unless his secretary sits right outside of his opened office door. Several years ago, he hired a godly woman who works full time to provide Christian counsel for the ladies in our church.

Not only do I need to be alert for potential danger, I want to be sensitive to the promptings of the Holy Spirit. I have found that, when being sensitive to Him, God will make me aware of needs, burdens, and challenges that I might otherwise have been oblivious to. I want to be the kind of wife who listens intently to God's Spirit and responds to His leading in my heart when it concerns the needs of my husband.

Practice a Spirit-filled Walk

We cannot be sensitive to the Holy Spirit if we are not maintaining a Spirit-filled walk. Walking in the Spirit is another critical key to supporting your husband. Ephesians 5:18–21 instructs us, *"And be not drunk with wine, wherein is excess; but be filled with the Spirit; Speaking to yourselves in psalms and hymns and spiritual songs, singing and making melody in your heart to the Lord; Giving thanks always for all things unto God and the Father in the name of our Lord Jesus Christ; Submitting yourselves one to another in the fear of God."* The word "filled" here means to be "controlled." Who or what controls you? Is God controlling you *today*? Right now? Or have you taken control of your life?

We would not experience as many problems in our homes and churches if we would only allow the Lord to take full control of every part of our lives on a daily basis. Our flesh doesn't want to give up control without a fight, so this is a daily struggle! We must die to self every day and continually practice a Spirit-filled walk. Learn to relinquish control in your home, your ministry, and your relationship. Give these areas to God and allow His Spirit to live through you as you serve Him.

A Spirit-filled wife will have a song in her heart. She will express thankfulness in all things. She will fear God and will exhibit a humble and yielded spirit. My husband keeps this prayer on the desk of his office:

A Yielded Spirit
Lord, I am willing to receive what YOU give,
to lack what YOU withhold, to relinquish what YOU take,
to suffer what YOU inflict, to be what YOU require,
and Lord, if others are to be YOUR messengers to me,
I am willing to hear and heed what they have to say.

Make this the prayer of your life! And, encourage your husband's heart by simply being a godly, Spirit-filled woman. It will make all the difference you need for your marriage and ministry!

Praise Him

Proverbs 12:25 says, *"Heaviness in the heart of man maketh it stoop: but a good word maketh it glad."*

One of the most important ways we can help our husbands reach their full potential is through frequent encouragement and praise. Proverbs 31:26 tells us of the virtuous woman: *"She openeth her mouth with wisdom; and in her tongue is the law of kindness."*

You have heard it said that the way to a man's heart is through his stomach. That may be one way to his heart, but I believe another route to his heart is through his ear! My husband always appreciates a good meal, but I notice the unique way he responds to a sincere word of encouragement or personal praise— and it far exceeds a good meal!

Men have affairs for many different reasons, but a common factor that influences men toward adulterous relationships is the lack of praise and the abundance of criticism from their wives. If a woman at work is quick to give your husband a compliment and his wife at home is just as quick to give a criticism, which one do you think he would be attracted to? No one (including your husband) wants to be rejected.

At the wedding altar, you vowed to become your husband's helpmeet—his cheerleader. Frankly, if you won't be that cheerleader, someone else *will* be.

Both of my daughters were cheerleaders, and both of my sons played sports. So I've been to quite a few high school athletic games! When the players made mistakes or missed points, I never heard the cheerleaders say, "You stupid team!" or "Even I could have made that basket!" Their cheers went more like this, "That's all right! That's okay! We're gonna win, anyway!" or "Stronger than steel, hotter than the sun, Bobby won't stop, 'til he gets the job done!" Just like the rest of us, your husband will make mistakes, but *you* choose your response. I encourage you to respond with cheers of encouragement. Lift him up. Support and strengthen him. Don't accentuate his weaknesses or failures, but cheer him on in spite of them!

Mark Twain said, "I can live two months on a good compliment." Everyone needs encouragement! If you feel like you may be weak in this area of praise, allow me to give you some ideas to get started.

Praise him for his person. First, encourage your husband for his person. The dictionary defines encouragement as "the expression of approval and support; or the act of giving hope or support to someone." Encouragement is realizing that a person has worth. God accepts him and loves him, why shouldn't you? Someone has said, "God loves each one of us as if there were only one of us."

Do your best to understand your husband. Listen to him, and look for ways to give plenty of support. We can give encouragement through words, through written notes, or by a touch or gesture. Send him a card. Give him a thumbs up, a wink, or a touch on the leg while you're in the car. Hold his hand while walking, and most of all, give him a smile! Who doesn't respond to a smile? Think of other special ways to encourage your husband, and be sure that whatever method of encouragement you choose communicates your complete acceptance of him!

If you are having trouble knowing how to praise your husband, think of what a woman would say to her man if she were trying to "steal him away," and say that to your husband!

Praise him for his provision for the family. God created man for work. Genesis 2:15 says, *"And the LORD God took the man, and put him into the garden of Eden to dress it and to keep it."* A man obtains a sense of identity from his job and takes his responsibility to provide very seriously. Show your husband that you appreciate his hard work and desire to provide.

When your husband is at work in the yard, notice what he accomplishes, take him a drink, and find something to do in the area where he is working. Then, show others his handiwork! Let him know in every way possible that you appreciate his hard labor.

The kids should show interest in their father's work as well. If your children are still young, remind them throughout the day that Daddy is at work helping people. Tell them that he is a hard worker and he takes such good care of the family.

When our kids were very little, we would take them by Caterpillar Machine Company. This company employed my husband while he worked his way through Bible college. As we drove by, we would make a big deal about how dad used to work there. Your husband *and* children will benefit from praising his work ethic.

Share his dreams. Another way to show support is by sharing his dreams. God has given my husband a tremendous vision for our marriage, our home, and our ministry. I've been given to him to support that vision and to share in his dreams! The last thing he needs me to do is laugh or dismiss the vision that God has placed on his heart. I want to be helpful, encouraging, and even influential in seeing his God-given vision become a reality!

A long time ago, I surrendered to the vision God gave to my husband. If I hadn't, I think I would be the most miserable woman alive today! His ministry vision and dreams are not his alone. They are mine too! We share them together. We pursue them together. My agenda is his agenda. I exist to support his dreams—and it truly is a wonderful life—together.

Few things will mean as much to your husband as when you lay aside your own pursuits to support his and when you surrender your dreams for God's. You'll find that God's plans for you and your husband together are far better than your own.

Compliment his preaching. People will tell your husband his message was too loud, too long, or too short. So he needs to hear some positive feedback from you! I'm not suggesting that you lie, but I am suggesting that you look for the good and praise it. Maybe you could sincerely say, "That message was just what I needed" or "I can tell the Lord really used that message today." When he preaches a great message, tell him so! Encourage him to preach that message if he is scheduled to preach in another ministry.

After a wedding ceremony, tell him it was beautiful and that you're thankful you are married to him. No one knows your husband like you do, and these sincere words coming from you will mean the world to him.

Praise your husband in the presence of your children. Remember your children need to know that dad is valuable and very important to the family. Some families treat the man of the house as excess baggage—almost as if he's not needed in the home and mom and the kids can handle it all. Teach your children that dad is not just a paycheck! Teach them to love, thank, and honor him!

Someone said, "Don't worry that children never listen to you; worry that they are always watching you." Our children notice how we, as parents, treat each other, and they emulate what they see. If you say you support and appreciate your husband, but your actions suggest otherwise, your children will not hear your words. They will see your actions.

Make your husband the family's hero!

Prepare a Peaceful Place

Another way to uplift the heart of your husband is by preparing a peaceful place for him when he comes home. Things may be falling apart in his world at work or in ministry, but let his home always be his relaxing retreat.

We've all heard that a man's home is his castle. I heard of one man who called his home a "trauma center." I thought that sounded horrible, but then he said, "It's where I go to become well again." That made more sense. You can call it what you like, but the truth is: our husbands need to come home to a place where their soul and body can be replenished, restored, and refreshed. Here are some actions we have tried to establish in the Chappell house. I pray that these ideas will be a blessing to *your* home.

Prepare to greet your husband. You have spent most of the day away from him, so those first few minutes when he gets home are the most crucial! How you welcome your mate seems to set the tone for the rest of the evening. (By the way, this is the love of your life, your best friend, your life's partner and companion—he is not just *anybody,* you know!)

First, stop what you are doing so you *can* greet him. Sometimes, I get so wrapped up in what I am working on that I barely give a nod of the head and a quick "hi" when my husband walks in the door. This is easy to do when you're busy, but resist the pattern. Put down the cooking utensils, and let your honey know you are glad to be with him again. Give him a smile, a kiss, and a hug. Spend a few moments simply enjoying his companionship. This time will serve as a prelude to a peaceful and enjoyable evening.

Get rid of the mess. Don't let clutter be his first encounter when he walks through the door. Clutter is confusion, and God is not the author of confusion! I know my husband cannot relax until the disorder is put back in place. So, take a few minutes before your husband arrives home to de-clutter.

- Have the kids do a quick pick up of their toys. Use a timer and make it a game to see how much can be cleaned up in five minutes.
- Do a five minute "room rescue" of the living/family room.
- De-clutter the kitchen. Wipe down the counters and sink with a little Pine-Sol or another good smelling cleaner.
- Keep a candle burning or better yet, have something cooking that smells good and says, "Welcome home!"
- Work as quickly as if company were on their way over. (It is amazing what you can do in just a few minutes with that mindset!)

I try to think of it this way: I want to cover all the senses for my husband. Touch—that's the hug and kiss. Sight—keeping the house picked up and presentable. Smell—have the house smelling clean and dinner smelling good. Taste—have dinner *tasting* good! Sound—put on some peaceful music and turn off the TV.

Tame the tots. When our kids were little, I often found myself trying to get dinner ready while simultaneously keeping the kids from tearing up the house—sometimes it was just plain chaos!

Getting dinner done earlier in the day by using a crock-pot or preparing a simple meal worked great for me and freed my time to settle down the children. I also tried to use the moments right before Dad came home as reading time. The kids enjoyed it, it relaxed all of us, and it sure impressed daddy to see everyone quietly reading a book when he walked through the door! If I was running late and reading wasn't an option, I would have the kids play a game— "who could see Daddy coming home first." They would all line up at the window and watch for Dad. This was a help to me as well, for when they yelled, "Daddy's home!" it gave me a quick minute to dry my hands and get ready to greet my husband. Of course, with this game, when Dad walked through the door, the kids always let him know we were glad he was home!

Play peaceful music. Music can soothe the soul. We see an example of this truth in the lives of Saul and David. First Samuel 16:23 says, *"And it came to pass, when the evil spirit from God was upon Saul, that David took an harp, and played with his hand: so Saul was refreshed, and was well, and the evil spirit departed from him."* William Gladstone said, "Music is one of the most forceful instruments for governing the mind and spirit of man." Music is powerful and can really help in setting the spirit of the home. (By the way, this is *not* the time for the kids to practice their instruments!)

Watch your words. Allow your husband to walk through the door and catch his breath before you unleash everything that happened to you that day—everything that went wrong, all the things he has to fix, everything the kids did, etc. Don't just throw the kids at him and say, "Your turn!"

Your words, and the tone in which you speak them, greatly affect your husband! What does God have to say about our speech? Read over this short list of verses:

> *She openeth her mouth with wisdom; and in her tongue is the law of kindness.*—PROVERBS 31:26

> *It is better to dwell in a corner of the housetop, than with a brawling woman in a wide house.*—PROVERBS 21:9

> *A continual dropping in a very rainy day and a contentious woman are alike.*—PROVERBS 27:15

> *Let no corrupt communication proceed out of your mouth, but that which is good to the use of edifying, that it may minister grace unto the hearers.*—EPHESIANS 4:29

> *A word fitly spoken is like apples of gold in pictures of silver.*—PROVERBS 25:11

*The Lord GOD hath given me the tongue of the learned, that
I should know how to speak a word in season to him that is
weary: he wakeneth morning by morning, he wakeneth mine
ear to hear as the learned.*—ISAIAH 50:4

*There is that speaketh like the piercings of a sword: but the
tongue of the wise is health.*—PROVERBS 12:18

But speaking the truth in love....— EPHESIANS 4:15

*A soft answer turneth away wrath: but grievous words stir up
anger. The tongue of the wise useth knowledge aright: but the
mouth of fools poureth out foolishness.*—PROVERBS 15:1–2

...for out of the abundance of the heart the mouth speaketh.
— MATTHEW 12:34

Have you ever been affected by what someone said, whether
it was good or bad? Have you ever been encouraged by kind
words? Have you ever been hurt by the words of someone else?
Have you ever been discouraged from doing a project because of a
negative comment? I know I have.

When a friend or classmate would say something cruel to me
as a child, I would always reply, "Sticks and stones may break my
bones, but words will never hurt me." But it wasn't true! Words
do hurt. Sometimes they hurt *more* than a broken bone, because a
bone will heal. Unkind words are remembered forever.

Words are powerful. They are not just letters attached
together; they are the manifestation of emotion. The words we
speak can give life, hope, and love—or they can tear down, divide,
and destroy. Proverbs 18:21 tells us that, *"Death and life are in the
power of the tongue...."* The taming of our tongue is so important
in our marriage and in our home.

Abigail Van Buren once wrote about a woman who listened
to a mother verbally destroy her child. The woman told the
mother, "I'll give you a dollar for him." It was only then that the
mother began to realize the value of her child. Do you realize the

value of your husband? Keep his significance in mind before you "go off" on him—belittling or berating him. Don't bombard him with questions, or worse—accusations when he walks through the door. Most moms have been talking to children all day and look forward to an adult conversation when their husbands come home. Most husbands have been with adults talking all day and look forward to a few minutes of peace and quiet when they get home. It didn't take me long to learn that my husband needs soft and kind words when he walks through the door at the end of a hard day. (And it didn't take me long to discover that just about every day is a hard day!)

At our house, we normally eat dinner as soon as my husband gets home. With a full tummy and a few minutes of peace, he is more willing to talk. So ladies, be patient. Give him a few quiet moments and a great dinner, and see if he isn't a little more ready to engage in some conversation!

We can talk to our husbands about things that are bothering us or important issues that need to be discussed, but we ought to pick the time, the place, and the tone we'll use for those important discussions. Here are guidelines to keep in mind while communicating with your husband:

- Attack the problem, not the person; even if you think the problem is the person! Avoid statements like, "you always" or "you never."

- Be careful of saying, "I'm just kidding." Most of the time we are not, and when we really are just kidding, they won't believe us.

- Think before you speak. James 1:19 says, "*Wherefore, my beloved brethren, let every man be swift to hear, slow to speak, slow to wrath.*"

- Hold your tongue when you are tempted to criticize, to correct him on a minor point of a story he is telling, or to say, "I told you so!"

- Ask God to let you hear yourself. Oftentimes, we have no idea how careless we are in our speech. Ask yourself, would I speak to him like that in front of _____? (Insert the name of someone you respect—Jesus; his parents; another pastor).

- Ask God to help you every day. Psalm 19:14 says, "*Let the words of my mouth, and the meditation of my heart, be acceptable in thy sight, O LORD, my strength, and my redeemer.*" Psalm 141:3 admonishes us to ask God to, "*Set a watch, O LORD, before my mouth; keep the door of my lips.*"

J. Sidlow Baxter said, "The proof that God's Spirit is in your life is not that you speak in an unknown tongue, but that you control the tongue you do know." Now that is convicting! Are you allowing God's Spirit to control your tongue? (Walking in the Spirit truly is the answer to being a good wife, isn't it?)

Listen lovingly. Listening is a great way to be supportive of your husband. Why do you think God gave us two ears and only one mouth? Could it be so that we would listen twice as much as we talk? Let's be honest, we all enjoy talking about ourselves or our ideas. But if you want to make an impact, listen as your hubby speaks about his life, his goals, and his dreams. Keep your eyes focused on *him* while he is talking. Remember that your listening is affirmation!

Perhaps you've heard this cute poem when you were younger:

> A wise old owl lived in an oak,
> The more he heard the less he spoke.
> The less he spoke, the more he heard,
> Why can't we all be like the wise old bird?

If we would just take the time to listen to our husbands, we might actually *learn* something! We might understand or even see his pain. We probably wouldn't jump to conclusions, and we would certainly grow closer to him.

George Eliot said, "Oh, the comfort, the inexpressible comfort of feeling safe with a person; having neither to weigh thoughts nor measure words, but to pour them all out, just as they are, chaff and grain together, knowing that a faithful hand will take and sift them, keep what is worth keeping, and then, with the breath of kindness, blow the rest away." Will you be that safe person for your husband? Will you strive to be one with whom he can be himself? Can he trust you to sift his words, understand his heart, and faithfully listen without rebuke? May this be the prayer of your heart as you lovingly listen to the man God has given to you.

Now, does this calm attitude or peaceful atmosphere take place every night at the Chappell home? I don't think so! But I *can* honestly say, it is the goal for which we strive! I pray you will attempt to maintain a peaceful place for your husband, as well. May our homes be a refuge and safe haven from the struggles of daily life, and may you praise and protect your husband as he leads your family and ministry!

CHAPTER THIRTEEN

Lifting Up the Heart of Your Husband: Part Two

God gave you to your husband as a minister of grace to his heart! I sincerely pray that it is your desire to uplift and strengthen him each and every day. Let's continue to examine some more ways that you can encourage your husband's heart.

Please Him—His Way

Men and women are so different! If my husband wanted to uplift the heart of his wife and be pleasing to me, he would bring me a huge bowl of real vanilla ice cream smothered in thick, rich hot fudge and lots of whipped cream! If he did this, I would be *very* pleased!

But, if I took my husband that same hot fudge sundae, he would let it melt. Okay, maybe not. But the point is, the gesture wouldn't convey the same message to him. What pleases me, doesn't necessarily please him.

Romans 12:10 tells us to *"Be kindly affectioned one to another with brotherly love; in honour preferring one another."* This verse doesn't just apply to our kindness toward friends and church members. God commands us to be kind to our *husbands* and to prefer them in honor! Always be on the lookout for ways you can please your husband.

Fun. After twenty-five years of marriage, my husband and I are more alike now in many of the ways in which we were different when we first got married. On the other hand, we can be total opposites too! Sometimes, when it comes to having a good time, we each have our own ideas about what is fun. For instance, my husband enjoys time on the golf course. I don't consider that fun. I enjoy walking through a mall (not even shopping—just looking). But that isn't even *close* to being fun for my husband. He says that you go to a mall only to buy something *needful*, and that the entire experience should last no more than ten minutes. Over the years, we have been on the golf course and in a shopping mall together numerous times. Why? Because we are preferring one another. I want to do what my husband considers to be fun because I love him, and I like to see him enjoying himself. And he feels the same way about me.

When we first got married, my husband liked basketball and I liked baseball. In our early years of marriage, we only went to baseball games. Then one year for Christmas, I decided to give my husband a "date-a-month." One of his monthly dates was to go to a professional basketball game. This was when the Lakers and the Celtics were the top two teams, and tickets were too expensive. Fortunately, the Clippers were in last place. So the only tickets I could get were for a Lakers vs. Clippers game, and the seats were up in the nosebleed section. I honestly didn't expect the evening to be much fun, but it turned out to be a blast! We both had a great time! I learned then that when I'm planning something fun for my husband, I can actually have fun too! (By the way, I'm hooked—I now love going to basketball games with my husband!)

You are your husband's recreational partner, and contrary to what you may think, he would rather be with you (when you have a good attitude) than with the guys! Go ahead and try doing some of those things that are enjoyable for your husband! You, too, may be surprised at how much fun you'll have.

Food. Consider your husband when deciding what you are going to make for dinner. He deserves to eat his favorite meals on more occasions than his birthday alone! My husband comes home to the dinner of my choice every evening. I pretty much get to prepare whatever I am in the mood for, and he never complains. But I don't want dinner to *always* be about what I feel like cooking. Dinner should be pleasing to him as well!

Also, buy the foods your husband enjoys. My entire family likes creamy peanut butter, except for—you guessed it—my husband! He loves super chunky. I could say, "We outnumber you!" I could just buy creamy and let him deal with it! Instead, I buy both, and when I'm making sandwiches for everyone, I have to get out two jars of peanut butter. (Now that's real sacrifice isn't it!?) Seriously, it's not that big of a deal! I want my husband to know that I care about what he likes, and that I buy those things just for him.

Fashion. Another way to please your husband his way is to dress the way he prefers for you to dress. Wear what your husband likes. If your husband doesn't like red, don't wear red. We should be dressing for our husband's compliments, not the compliments of another woman or man.

If you are able to be at home all day, don't stay in your robe the entire time! It might even be nice to get dressed *before* he goes to work. When he leaves in the morning, he takes that image with him throughout the day. How do you want him to remember you?

Finances. Many couples will agree that this area can cause a lot of marital grief! Pastor's wives, don't forget your husband carries not only the burden of the household finances, but he also carries the burden of the church's finances. Don't add to that burden. Desire to help him, even in the area of finances.

Does your husband want you to use a check, ATM card, or cash? What receipts does he want you to keep and where? Chuck Bowen, a Christian finance coach, said one of the most common feelings expressed to him when working with couples is this, "If I could just get my spouse to work with me, then we could really make some headway!" Find out what will please your husband and what could be a help to him and then incorporate that into your routine.

Keep Passion Alive and Exciting

Let the husband render unto the wife due benevolence: and likewise also the wife unto the husband. The wife hath not power of her own body, but the husband: and likewise also the husband hath not power of his own body, but the wife. Defraud ye not one the other, except it be with consent for a time, that ye may give yourselves to fasting and prayer; and come together again, that Satan tempt you not for your incontinency.
—1 Corinthians 7:3–5

Most of us naturally ensure that our own needs are met. But it takes a deliberate effort—an act of the will, a choice—to focus instead on meeting the needs of our husbands.

I often hear women say, "My needs are not being met." It seems the more we focus on getting *our* needs met, the more frustrated and unfulfilled we are. The more I try to meet the needs of my husband, the more my own needs are fulfilled! I can't explain it. It is one of those Bible principles that doesn't make sense to our human minds. God blesses you when you die to self and live for another. The Bible is filled with these paradoxes—the way up is down, the first shall be last, and give and it shall be given unto you! The world says, "Look out for number one." The Bible says, *"And as ye would that men should do to you, do ye also to them likewise"* (LUKE 6:31).

On the wedding day, both husband and wife make exclusive promises that they will meet each other's needs, and that they will only allow these needs to be met by their spouse. A husband has needs that can *only* be met by his wife. We must give ourselves to understanding those needs and learning to meet them.

Remember that it is impossible to meet every one of your husband's needs, and it is impossible for him to meet every one of yours. Yet we can give ourselves to meeting those within our power. Most marriage books list the husband's need for physical intimacy in the top five needs of every man, and most wives would probably not put that need at the top of the list! Men have a God-given, built in need for physical intimacy, much like *we* do for air, food, or *chocolate*! It is a real need and there are some ways to meet that need and to keep that passion alive in your marriage.

By being interested. Express the kind of interest in your husband that you expressed when you dated him. Be interested in what your husband is interested in.

We sat together for lunch on our first date in Bible college. My husband-to-be asked if I would like to see pictures from Korea. I thought they would be pictures of his family, but not one person showed up in any of those photos! For a long time, we looked at photos of Korean wild flowers. Yet it was interesting to me because it was interesting to him! I have sat through some long golf tournaments. I don't exactly like golf, but I love being with my husband. I've tried to express an interest in what interests him.

We should also show interest in the area of intimacy. Meeting his need in this area is more than just "putting up with his advances" or "just going through the motions." He needs to know that his wife is interested and that he is satisfying her. Remember this is a God-given gift meant to be enjoyed and shared together.

By initiating. Women often comment to me that they don't date their husbands anymore. Usually, I respond by asking,

"When was the last time *you* planned a date?" You are married! It is not only *okay* to flirt with your husband—it is *needful*! Better than planning a date is planning to steal him away for a couple of days! To tell you the truth, I have more fun planning and preparing a secret getaway than if my husband had done it for me. Try it!

If your husband travels, why not pick him up from the airport from time to time? Sometimes I will do this, and rather than taking him straight back to church and to the pressures of the day, I steal him away for a few hours and let him know how glad I am that he is home!

Many books have been written on the differences between men and women, so I won't spend a lot of time discussing these distinctions. But I do want to mention one. For most women, when it comes to intimacy, we want everything to be just perfect. If we're dealing with stress, pressure, or fatigue, the last thing on our mind is what is on our husband's mind! But for most men, it is the opposite. The times when your husband is under pressure, fatigue, or additional stress are the times when he needs this physical attention the most. If the Holy Spirit allows you to see these extra burdens, then it's time to take the initiative and meet your husband's needs.

By investing. The definition of *invest* is, "to commit in order to gain profit or interest." A guaranteed way to increase your love for someone is to invest time in that person. Begin by doing special acts of kindness for your husband, and you will find that your love for him will thrive. Love is not only an emotion, it is a decision—an act of the will. When a wife *decides* to act in loving ways towards her husband, the feelings will soon follow. There must be continual dating, expressions of affection, and kindness to keep love alive and flourishing. Some actions to rekindle your love for your husband could be:

+   Pray.
+   Say "I love you" often.

- Buy or write him romantic cards.
- Get up earlier than your husband and surprise him by putting toothpaste on his toothbrush.
- On a cold morning, warm his towel in the dryer while he is taking a shower.
- Leave love notes around the house.
- Think of him in loving ways.
- Rub his back.
- Put lotion on his feet.
- Give him romantic looks.
- Flirt with him.
- Hug him often.
- Kiss him romantically.
- Let him know you are interested in him romantically.

In addition to investing acts of kindness, invest time and money into keeping yourself as attractive as possible. You should also invest in some good reading material on marriage and on the home. Lastly, invest some money into a good babysitter and be sure to get time just to yourselves!

Pay Attention to the Tiny Details

When we were first married, I did the banking. We did not have automatic deposits, and we worked out of one checkbook. On Mondays, I would go to the bank and make a deposit, and each week I would forget to write down the deposit. No big deal, we always had more in the bank than I wrote down on paper! My husband didn't see it that way. He wanted the check balance written down, and he wanted it correct! One particular Monday, I remembered to write down the deposit, but later in that same week I forgot that I had already recorded the deposit. You guessed it—I entered that deposit a second time! Two weeks went by and we got a little notice in the mail that we had bounced a check. We couldn't figure out why. We still had plenty of money in our account according to our ledger. After some research, my husband brought to my attention that I recorded one deposit twice! That little tiny detail cost us a great deal. (By the way, the check that bounced was to our church!)

> *I will remember the works of the LORD: surely I will remember thy wonders of old.*—Psalm 77:11

> *Take us the foxes, the little foxes, that spoil the vines: for our vines have tender grapes.*—Song of Solomon 2:15

One hundred forty-six times in God's Word we're told to remember. Remembering must take a high priority with God, and when it comes to uplifting your husband's heart, remembering plays a big role.

We have all heard the saying, "The little things mean the most." This statement could not be truer than in the realm of marriage. It would greatly benefit most husbands and wives if we would just remember to practice this old wise saying. So often we forget to do the little things that mean the most. Here are some ways I encourage you to remember your husband:

- You are his helpmeet—so don't forget the obvious and help him every way you can.
- Make your husband look good in public. Don't correct him or criticize him.
- No PDB—public display of bickering!
- Say "thank you" for even the tiniest kindness.
- Make your time together count. Don't spend time telling your husband you never get to spend time together.
- Keep dating. After you are married it is okay to ask your husband for a date, or better yet, get away for a day or two.
- Make sure he has clean clothes. I can be busy doing a lot of great things, but if my husband says he doesn't have any clean socks, I have failed. I confess this happened more than once in our family. Now I keep a spare set of clothing in my closet just for those times that I get behind!
- Sunday is his biggest day of the week—allow him some quiet time on Saturday to study and to prepare for Sunday. I tease

my husband and tell him he has PMS—every Saturday
—pre-message syndrome!

♦   Do things for him he doesn't expect.

*Through wisdom is an house builded; and by understanding it is
established: And by knowledge shall the chambers be filled with
all precious and pleasant riches.*—PROVERBS 24:3–4

Provide Forgiveness

In the secular world, forgiveness has become a lost art. People
have the attitude that someone has to pay for their hurt. People
want revenge on the person that upset them. Every day we hear
on the news that someone is suing someone else, often over some
trivial offense. Unfortunately, this attitude has crept into the lives
of Christians. I have heard Christians say, "I just can't forgive"
and even more sadly, "I won't forgive." In our marriages when
we should be loving and caring, we are often bitter because of an
unforgiving spirit. May I admonish you right now? Don't hold on
to grudges for the offenses of your husband. Your grudge will not
only hurt your marriage, it will destroy you as well.

Someone said, "Men forget everything, women remember
everything." That's why men need instant replays in sports.
They've already forgotten what happened! Someone else said, "A
married man should forget his mistakes. There's no use in two
people remembering the same thing!"

The truth of the matter is this: every marriage is made up of
two sinners, but every *great* marriage is made up of two forgivers.
Let's look at some facts about forgiveness.

Forgiving is not forgetting! I remember hearing adults
say, "Let's just forgive and forget." It didn't take me long before I
realized that, while it is *hard* to forgive, it is *impossible* to forget!
When I was expecting our first child, I remember asking my mom
about labor. She said, "Oh, it hurts, but when the baby is born you
forget about the pain." I'm not sure what she was talking about,

because it's been twenty-four years since Danielle was born, and I *still* remember the pain! Do you know what my mom meant? She meant that the pain I experienced at the time of Danielle's birth was all encompassing; it was controlling; it was all I could think of in that moment. But after she was born, that pain no longer had control over me. It was replaced by a far greater delight and joy!

This is what happens when you forgive. Truly forgiving someone does not mean that you have forgotten the hurt. It does mean, however, that the pain of the offense no longer has control over you.

I am so thankful that God has forgiven me. God chooses not to remember my sins. Hebrews 8:12 says, *"For I will be merciful to their unrighteousness, and their sins and their iniquities will I remember no more."* When God says he will remember no more, I don't think He means He is literally forgetting. I believe He is choosing not to recall my sins to His mind. Forgiving is not forgetting, but it's simply letting go of the hurt.

Forgiveness does not demand revenge. God is the righteous judge and He will make everything right. Don't manipulate or scheme to "get even." Simply leave your bitterness at the cross and trust God for the outcome.

Forgiveness is a decision. Forgiveness is a conscious choice—a decision to let an offense go and to let the offender off the hook. When our son, Larry, was a toddler, he loved to play with rocks. One afternoon he went fishing with my dad, and after only a few minutes of fishing, Larry decided that he would rather play with rocks than fish. So with little advance notice he began throwing rocks into the water, which in turn was scaring off all the fish. My dad had to think quickly before Larry ruined any chance of a catch! He hurried to the motor home and came out a moment later with ice cream. You can imagine what my son did. Without a second thought, he dropped two fistfuls of rocks and opted for ice cream!

God wants to give us freedom from our pain, our bitterness, and our frustration, but we can't accept God's blessing if we are clinging to the rocks of bitterness. It is impossible to inhale new air until you exhale the old, and in marriage it is impossible to experience the wonderful, blessed relationship of intimacy and love that God desires to give you if you are holding on to the offenses of your husband.

Clara Barton, the founder of the American Red Cross, is a terrific example of someone who was never known to hold a grudge against anyone. One time a friend reminded her of a cruel accusation that someone had made against her years earlier, but Clara seemed not to remember the incident. "Don't you remember the wrong that was done to you?" the friend asked. "No," Clara answered calmly. "I distinctly remember forgetting that."

Do not expect that your decision to forgive will result in changes in the other person, but do expect positive results of forgiveness within you. Sometimes when we say "you are forgiven," we are really saying "I will forgive you if you will change and never commit the offense again." That doesn't always happen and that's not true forgiveness. When we forgive, we don't change the past and we don't change the future deeds of another person, but we sure do change the future of our own hearts.

Forgiveness is not a *feeling*. Don't confuse forgiveness as an emotion. It is a commitment. It is a choice! If you are struggling in this area of forgiveness towards your husband, here are some tips:

- *Pray.* Ask God to enable you to forgive.

- *Ask.* Ask the Lord to help you see your husband as He sees him.

- *Share.* Calmly and honestly share your pain with your husband.

- ◆ *Commit.* Commit to repeated forgiveness. Matthew 18:21–22 says, *"Then came Peter to him, and said, Lord, how oft shall my brother sin against me, and I forgive him? till seven times? Jesus saith unto him, I say not unto thee, Until seven times: but, Until seventy times seven."*

- ◆ *Focus on the cross.* Ephesians 4:32 says, *"And be ye kind one to another, tenderhearted, forgiving one another, even as God for Christ's sake hath forgiven you."* Colossians 3:13 commands that, *"Forbearing one another, and forgiving one another, if any man have a quarrel against any: even as Christ forgave you, so also do ye."*

Don't ever forget that God forgave you! Your husband could not possibly offend you as badly as you have offended God. We nailed our Saviour to the cross. If He can forgive us, then we can forgive another.

Conclusion

The Taj Mahal is one of the most beautiful and costly tombs ever built, but there is something fascinating about its beginnings. In 1629, when the favorite wife of Indian ruler Shah Jahan died, he ordered that a magnificent tomb be built as a memorial to her. The Shah placed his wife's casket in the middle of a parcel of land, and construction of the temple literally began around it. But several years into the venture, the shah's grief for his wife gave way to a passion for the project. One day while he was surveying the sight, he reportedly stumbled over a wooden box, and he had some workers throw it out. It was months before he realized that the box was his wife's casket, and it had been destroyed. The original purpose for the memorial became lost in the details of construction.

You are building something much more important than the Taj Mahal! You are building a marriage, a family, a life-long love relationship. Don't become so busy with the details of living that you lose sight of your God-given husband *and* of your God-given responsibility as a wife to encourage him!

We've studied nine ways to uplift your husband's heart:

- By praying for him
- By protecting him
- By practicing a Spirit-filled walk
- By praising him
- By preparing a peaceful place
- By pleasing him—his way
- By keeping passion alive and exciting
- By paying attention to the tiny details
- By providing forgiveness

As we conclude these important chapters, I hope you will ask the Lord to help you become the helpmeet that your husband needs. I pray that you will change your perspective, if needed, and make it your purpose in life to glorify God by uplifting the heart of the man He has given to you.

CHAPTER FOURTEEN

Given to Hospitality

Use hospitality one to another without grudging.
—1 Peter 4:9

What goes through your mind when you hear the word "hospitality"? Is your first thought, "That's not for me!"? Do you lapse in fear at the thought of having people into your home? Do you feel insecure because you don't know where to start? Do you have visions of all the possible "disasters" that could take place in the kitchen? Do you feel overwhelmed by the thought of adding another event to your already busy schedule? Me too! Let's skip this chapter….

Okay, that would be convenient, but since the Lord has commanded us to be "given to hospitality," maybe we should just submit to His plan and see what happens.

When considering hospitality, perhaps different types of thoughts came to your mind; or, maybe all of these thoughts came flooding through your mind. If so, I can identify with you!

I was first introduced to hospitality two weeks after I was married. My husband had preached his first sermon as a married pastor in a hot, desert city in Southern California—Bombay Beach (it was located nowhere near an ocean and about a hundred miles from everything!). After the morning service, one of the ladies of the church invited us over for lunch. Since the closest restaurant was an hour away and we didn't have any money, we were more than happy to accept. This woman's husband was not a Christian, so we were also praying that God would allow us to use this time of fellowship to share the Gospel with him.

As soon as we were seated, the husband of our hostess announced that they would be serving leftovers. Now, please don't get me wrong. I am totally okay with leftovers. I actually even like leftovers better than the original meal sometimes! It was when the husband said he hoped we wouldn't get botulism from the two-week-old lasagna that my stomach began to churn slightly. At first I thought he was joking, so I began to laugh. But, he was not laughing, nor did he take any lasagna as it was passed. In fact, he made cutting comments about each dish that went by.

I desperately began searching for *something* safe to eat when my eye spotted a 9 x 13 pan of Jell-O topped with Cool Whip on a TV tray at the corner of the table. I thought to myself, "I don't care how long that has been in the refrigerator! You can't ruin Jell-O, and that's what I'm going to eat!"

When our hostess reached for the dish of Jell-O, I watched as she turned slightly and blew over the top of the dish. I continued to watch in disbelief as white dog hair went flying off the top of the Jell-O and onto the floor. It wasn't Cool Whip that I saw. It was dog hair from her five white Alaskan Huskies that lived *in* the house! My stomach couldn't handle any more, so I ran into the restroom. As I was trying to regain my composure, I promised myself that I would never treat company like that in my home. I determined right then and there that I would make our guests feel special and loved. I would do my best to be a gracious hostess.

My first official attempt at gracious hospitality came a few months later at a different ministry, and it was not what I imagined it to be. My husband had just started a couples' class, and he was so excited the Sunday our first visiting couple attended church. Imagine my shock when, right in the middle of class, he invited them over to our home for lunch! I immediately thought, "This is not good!" I was expecting our second child and was not feeling very pleasant or hospitable. We also did not have any food at home! (In fact, I was praying someone would have *us* over for Sunday lunch that day!) By the time our class was over, I was convinced that he had not been serious in his invitation.

As we walked home from church, I reached for my husband's hand and said, "I'm so glad you were teasing about having people over today. I was really worried for a minute there!" It was when he assured me that he was *not* joking that I looked behind my shoulder and saw the visiting couple following us to our apartment!

My brain quickly began to formulate a plan. The closest store was a 7-Eleven on the corner of our street, and we only had seven dollars. I ran to the 7-Eleven with the little money we had and bought a package of spaghetti noodles, a can of green beans, and a half-gallon of ice cream (no meal is complete without dessert, right?). So, our big Sunday afternoon meal and my first debut in hospitality consisted of buttered noodles, green beans and ice cream.

To my surprise, the couple joined the church the next Sunday! (I think it was the ice cream!)

Examining the Biblical Principle

The Bible is clear that we should be given to hospitality. In fact, it is one of the qualifications for a pastor.

A bishop then must be blameless, the husband of one wife,
vigilant, sober, of good behaviour, given to hospitality, apt to
teach."—1 Timothy 3:2

Now, my husband has no problem being given to hospitality, but he can't do it by himself! He needs my help! And, your husband needs yours. So many wives hinder their husband's ministry by dragging their feet in this area. The Bible even goes so far as to say that we are to be hospitable without complaining. First Peter 4:9 says, *"Use hospitality one to another without grudging."* This means we should not complain over the inconvenience of hosting company, the time involved in preparation, our inadequate furnishings, or the added expense or burden.

So what exactly *is* hospitality? According to the dictionary, it is the "cordial and generous reception of or disposition toward guests." According to the Bible, it is a ministry to others in the name of Jesus Christ.

For whosoever shall give you a cup of water to drink in my name,
because ye belong to Christ, verily I say unto you, he shall not lose
his reward.—Mark 9:41

Hospitality is not entertainment. This truth has been expressed many ways:

+ Hospitality is a safe place, entertainment is a show place.

+ The important thing is not what is on the table, but who occupies the chairs.

+ Hospitality focuses on people, entertainment focuses on things.

Our goal in hospitality should not be to *impress* our guests, but to *express* our love—the love of Christ. The key to practicing hospitality is to forget yourself and to remember your guests.

It seems as though our society doesn't have time to be hospitable. Fast food restaurants have long lines full of people who don't want to eat at home, much less invite someone over for a meal. Our lives are often too busy to reach out to someone else, and we tend to focus on our own needs much more than we do on the needs of others.

Yet, as servants of Christ, God wants us to be lovers of hospitality. Titus 1:8 says, *"But a lover of hospitality, a lover of good men, sober, just, holy, temperate."* We should not be hospitable because we are *required* to, but because we allow the Holy Spirit to give us that desire—to help us to *want* to. I've discovered that true hospitality is an attitude of the heart. Ask God to help you be willing to open your heart and home to those whom you are called to minister.

> *Let brotherly love continue. Be not forgetful to entertain strangers: for thereby some have entertained angels unawares.*
> —HEBREWS 13:1–2

> *Distributing to the necessity of saints; given to hospitality.*
> —ROMANS 12:13

Examples of Biblical Hospitality

God, in His Word, not only commands us to be hospitable, He gives us examples of those who were given to hospitality. One of my favorite examples of hospitality is the husband and wife team of Aquila and Priscilla. In Acts 18, the Bible says Paul abode with Aquila and Priscilla on his missionary journey.

Jesus was a guest in the house of Zacchaeus in Luke 19 and in the home of Mary and Martha in Luke 10.

Abraham and Sarah are also great examples of hospitality. In Genesis 18, we see how Abraham served his guests. He first welcomed them, and then made them comfortable by washing their feet and giving them a place to rest. Abraham asked his wife Sarah to prepare a meal—and a large one at that! Abraham and Sarah were wonderful hosts. Little did they know, they had *"entertained angels unawares"* (Hebrews 13:2).

Other Old Testament examples include Rahab in Joshua 2, who secretly lodged two spies. Abigail fed David and his men in 1 Samuel 25. In 1 Kings 17, we see the widow of Zarephath sustaining Elijah with the only food in her house. Another favorite of mine is the Shunammite woman of 2 Kings 4. The Bible says she was perceptive. She thought of everything she could do for her guest, Elisha. I thank God for these Bible characters who challenge me to be hospitable out of a heart of love for the Lord!

Effects of Hospitality

The rewards of hospitality are plentiful. First, hospitality strengthens our relationships. Just as our family ties are made stronger when we host immediate or extended families for a special holiday meal, so our relational ties are strengthened with our church family when we welcome them into our homes for Christ-centered fellowship. There is a unique bonding that usually takes place when we open up our homes and share our lives with others.

Hospitality is a tremendous tool for discipling new Christians. What a great opportunity it is for a young Christian to see what a "real" Christian home is like! What a training and mentoring momen that is for themt! They should experience gathering around a table to pray before a meal. They should see God's Word in a prominent place and hear good, godly music. They shouldn't see things in the home that would hinder their Christian walk. (For example, liquor and inappropriate videos or reading material will have a negative effect on their spiritual growth.) We should be careful not to put a stumblingblock in the way of a young Christian. Romans 14:13 says, *"Let us not therefore judge one another any more: but judge this rather, that no man put a stumblingblock or an occasion to fall in his brother's way."*

Hospitality also gives us the opportunity to get to know church members better. Having someone into your home allows time for more than a casual hello or polite wave across the church auditorium. As we spend time in fellowship, we can share in their blessings and we can pray for their burdens. We can be a source of encouragement to those who are experiencing a difficult time. This "one-on-one" time also gives us the privilege to encourage spiritual growth. Oftentimes, people open up easier and feel more comfortable asking questions in our home than they would during a meeting or event at church. Ultimately, having guests in your home will increase your friendship and strengthen your relationship with those in the church.

As a mom, I appreciate the learning experiences my children receive by having guests into our home. From the example we set as parents, they will learn how to serve and how to share. They will learn manners, proper etiquette, and good behavior (hopefully!). Opening our home helped our children overcome shyness. It also helped them learn how to interact with children and adults. They have been exposed to all types of people in our home, from the unsaved person needing God's gift of salvation, to the young Christian who is bursting with questions, to the missionary or pastor who is faithfully serving the Lord.

Over the years, we have invited missionaries into our home after the evening services of our missions conferences. My children began to appreciate the work of the ministry as they literally sat at the feet of great men of God who shared interesting stories and exciting updates. So it didn't surprise me when our daughter, Kristine, surrendered at a young age to be a missionary. She continues to have a special burden for the mission field and for our missionaries. You will be thankful for the positive impact hospitality will have on your family.

Second, hospitality helps you realize what is really important in life. Things are not important—people are. By striving to be an encouragement to others through hospitality, you will inevitably receive encouragement in return. Are you willing to put yourself in a position to experience that blessing?

There's a song that we've sung in our church a few times that simply says, "We've been blessed to be a blessing. We've been loved to give His love." The song ends by saying that "the greatest in His kingdom is the servant of us all." Friend, God has blessed you with many things, and He desires for you to use those blessings to bless others—to express the love of Christ to those within your reach.

Eliminating the Excuses

Before we can begin to practice hospitality, we have to get rid of the excuses! George Washington Carver said, "Ninety-nine percent of the failures come from people who have the habit of making excuses." Below I've listed several "excuses" that I've heard over the years for not exercising hospitality.

We are too busy. There's an old proverb that says, "You always have time to do the things you want to do." I believe that truth is applicable here. If you truly desire to have people into your home, then you must schedule a time to do it! We have most of our company over after evening services. This works great for us because we already know there is nothing else planned. Also, it doesn't take away from another night at home with the family.

I don't have a big enough house. The size of the house is really not an issue. We have lived in some pretty small spaces and that hasn't hindered us from having people over. We just had to become creative. Necessity is the mother of invention, right?

When we first moved to Lancaster, the small duplex we lived in did not have a working stove. The eating area only consisted of a very small table in the kitchen, but we still had people over. I used a crockpot and an electric skillet, and we ate at the living room coffee table. Obviously, you may not be able to have twenty people over in small conditions like that, but you can still host a few.

Ladies often hear how many people we have over now and think that they have to have a large group over to be considered "hospitable." But, we didn't start with large groups! We began with one family at a time, and God has done the rest.

The house is a mess. What better motivation for keeping your house clean than to know company is coming! I chuckle when I think of mothers who tell their children to clean their rooms, and the childrens' first response is, "Who's coming over?"! Hopefully, we don't clean our house just when company is coming, but having a clean home is definitely conducive to an enjoyable time of fellowship.

Don't feel like you have to bleach your entire house every other day to have people into your home. Keep in mind that people are not coming to your house to inspect for dirt or dust bunnies. I have not yet had anyone do a white glove inspection on my furniture! God wants us to keep our homes clean and in order, but your house does not need to be so immaculate and intimidating that people would be afraid to make themselves comfortable.

One experience certainly drove this point home for me. The day after Thanksgiving is our traditional time to decorate for Christmas! Our family eagerly anticipates this time together as we play Christmas music, eat left-over turkey, decorate the tree, and hang the various decorations we've collected over the years.

This particular year, we had just moved into a new home, so we were having trouble knowing where to store Thanksgiving decorations and where to put all of our Christmas décor. We had Thanksgiving decorations hanging out of various boxes all across the hallway, the dining room table, the kitchen table, and the kitchen counter. All of the coffee tables were covered with Christmas decorations that had been strewn about by the children. (This also happened to be after a Thanksgiving in which we hosted over fifty people in our home. All the leftover food was underneath the decorations on the kitchen counter.)

You can imagine my shock, then, when my husband brought a visiting pastor over—unannounced! This was the absolute worst time to be surprised with company!

When my husband and his guest walked in the door, there was nothing I could do! There was more than five minutes worth of straightening to be done. So, we just apologized for the mess and offered him something to eat—a casserole from all the left-over Thanksgiving food. (I found out later that this man hates for his foods to touch! He loathes casseroles!) But he received a welcoming spirit, a warm meal, and a personal glimpse into the decorating tradition of the Chappell family!

Again, purposely allowing your house to be continually dirty or unkept is not pleasing to the Lord. But God can use your hospitality to be a blessing to others, even if the situation is unexpected or doesn't seem to be perfect!

I'm not a good cook. We are so fortunate to live in the twenty-first century! We are able to shop at stores like Sam's Club where we can buy a lot of semi-homemade foods that require very little cooking or preparation. Plus, most supermarkets carry a lot of prepared foods, such as: roasted chicken (that can be used in so many recipes), bakery items, fruit and vegetable trays, and deli meats. If preparing an entire meal doesn't work for you, invite your guests over for: popcorn and soda; pie and coffee; or cake and ice cream.

You may also want to practice on your family by making some easy recipes and perfecting them. I try to use recipes with foods that most people don't make for themselves. This way, they won't compare it to the one they make, and (hopefully) it will be a treat for them.

We can't afford it. We put entertaining in our budget. Remember, you don't have to budget for or prepare gourmet meals. Early on, I learned to make dishes that were more economical. For many years I served homemade soup, fresh-baked bread, and brownies for dessert. It was very cost efficient, and our guests loved it.

Save money by taking advantage of good sales and stocking up on items you can use in the future. My mom taught me to take five dollars from my food budget (that was awhile ago, so you may want to increase that amount!) and buy five dollars worth of whatever was on sale, whether I needed it or not. That advice has helped me many times and has allowed us to serve a variety of meals over the years.

I don't have nice china and crystal. I don't want to come across as too simplistic, but it doesn't bother *me* what kind of dish I eat on as long as it's clean! And it probably doesn't bother most people as well. So use what you have! Try serving buffet style. It is more informal, and people don't expect to see nice china on a buffet table.

It seems I never have enough matching silverware, so I just try to have the pieces that do match at the same place setting. Besides, I know a lot of people with gorgeous china and they don't ever use it!

My husband doesn't want company. Even if your husband does not want to have people over, you can still be hospitable. Perhaps you can invite mothers over for muffins and coffee after they drop their kids off at school. Invite ladies over for lunch. What lady wouldn't enjoy talking over dessert and tea in the afternoon? Look for ways to fit hospitality into your schedule for times that would not inconvenience your family.

I've discovered that if you wait until you have time to prepare gourmet meals, served on beautiful china, in a spotless (including the cupboards), quiet home, you'll never do it! So, don't wait until your circumstances are perfect to reach out to others. Instead, ask God to show you ways to nurture your friendships using what He has given you. God doesn't expect you to use what He has not provided, but He does expect you to do the very best you can with everything that He has given you. When you do this, you open the door for God to do more. Why would God bless you with more if you're not using what He has already given to you for His glory?

Establishing a Plan

Practicing Christian hospitality isn't about being a Martha Stewart or a Betty Crocker. It's more important than that! It is about loving others and making people feel special. Our theme verse for our church this year is Philippians 4:13, and it's a great verse for Christian wives. *"I can do all things through Christ which strengtheneth me."* This even includes having people in your home! So begin planning!

Plan ahead. You will be more inclined to practice hospitality if you have a plan of action. Decide in advance when you will have people over. Do not overwhelm yourself; hospitality does not have to involve a lot of time and effort. Don't make it harder than it is!

Mark the calendar. "If you fail to plan, then you are planning to fail." Bear in mind, you don't have to have people over every other night! Don't psyche yourself into thinking you have to have company after every service. Start by setting aside one Sunday night a month. Since you are doing the inviting, choose a date when there's not much planned before or after.

Plan who to invite. Let me emphasize it again: don't think you have to have large groups over to be considered hospitable. When we first began having people into our home, we started with one or two people. It soon became natural for us to have people over. It got to the point that my husband and I felt like we were scheduling people a year in advance, so I suggested that we begin inviting groups over. If my house is all ready for company and I am cooking for eight, I can cook for fifteen without too much extra work.

As a family, make a list of people who would be especially encouraged by an invitation. As our children became teenagers, we let them in on the process. This way, they looked forward to having company and they had someone to fellowship with as well.

Invite different people in your church family. We rarely invite the same families over and over again. We try to invite as many different people into our home as possible. We invite visitors, new members, and long-time members. Sometimes, we invite people of the same Sunday school class or people who serve in the same ministry together. This will broaden the chance for everybody to have something to talk about. If you would like to invite a new acquaintance but aren't sure you have enough in common to keep a conversation going, ask another couple to join you.

Plan what to serve. Stick to meals and recipes that are easy! When you're hosting, it is not the time to bring out the most complicated recipes. Why put yourself through that? I keep a notebook of easy and tasty recipes that my family and others enjoy. I also have menu plans in the notebook that have worked well for me, and a shopping list that goes along with those menus. When my family gets tired of them, I look for new ideas.

Plan the details. Decide if you are going to have a nice, sit-down dinner, family-style meal, or a buffet. If we have a large group over, we almost always serve buffet style.

I try to prepare as much as possible ahead of time. I do this by setting the table the night before, cleaning as much as I can the day before, and preparing much of the meal the day before.

Remember that you don't have to do it all yourself. You can enlist teens or other ladies to help. Of course, enlist your family to help! When someone offers to bring something for big events or holiday meals, I let them. We usually have a lot of church members and college students into our home for Thanksgiving. I always ask the church members to bring whatever makes it "Thanksgiving" for them. If you have other staff ladies, perhaps you could enlist their help. Be creative, and make it a team effort.

Planning ahead makes things run more smoothly, but there will still be times when something will go wrong. I have had my share of those times! There have been a few occasions when I've rushed home after a service and didn't smell a thing—that is a bad sign!

One Sunday afternoon, we had Dr. David Gibbs into our home. For some reason, the oven did not turn on while we were at church, so the meat did not finish cooking. By the time I served dinner, it was still very tough. I was so embarrassed! Dr. Gibbs, being the kind person he is, kept saying, "Don't worry, Miss

Terrie, I like chewy meat." Now, I know better than that! No one likes chewy meat! I was humiliated at the moment, but I lived through it! And, it has brought several opportunities for laughter and teasing since! Now if something starts to go wrong before company walks in the door, my daughters remind me of that episode. The memory eases my nerves and brings fun back to serving others!

In an effort to make it through potential disasters, just imagine the worst thing that can happen and decide in advance how you will deal with that possibility.

Another way to plan the details is to remember the preferences of your guests. Organization is not my finest quality, but I do try to keep a record of what people like to drink. I also jot down any special health needs or allergies. We have a few guests that come through once or twice a year. If I know they are diabetic, I will serve sugar-free foods, for instance. You can also record what you served, what they liked, and what you shouldn't make again! This just takes a little time, but it makes your guests feel special and helps relieve some stress on your part.

Efficient and Practical Tips

- Keep several proven recipes and the ingredients to make them on hand.
- Stock up on convenience foods (like brownie mix), especially when they are on sale.
- When cooking and baking, make extra and freeze for later.
- Buy hamburger and chicken in bulk. Brown the meat all at once and freeze in individual freezer bags. For last-minute guests, I can make taco soup, nachos, or spaghetti sauce, and I won't dirty my stove.
- Try to keep at least the living room and bathroom clean at all times.
- Think of questions to ask ahead of time to keep the conversation going.

    —How did you and your husband meet?

    —How did you hear about our church?

    —Ask them to give their testimony.

    —Ask about their children.

- Concentrate on people, not preparations.
- Use candles to keep things smelling nice. There is something about a pleasant smell that is inviting. Candles also create a pleasant atmosphere.
- Pray. Ask God to bless the time of fellowship. Pray that your guests will feel His presence in your home. Don't forget to pray for the details! When my children were babies, I asked God to keep them full, dry, and content while our guests were over. And I always pray that the food will taste good!
- Set the table the night before. This is one less detail to concern yourself with the day of.
- Have Christian music playing quietly as guests arrive.
- Keep a sense of humor and lose any sense of pride.
- Remember, it's all in the attitude.
- Use placemats and cloth napkins to add more warmth and "homeyness."
- Reach out to others on special holidays—especially to those who have no family near them.
- Pass food to the left. It's always clockwise.
- Food is served from the left and plates are removed from the right.
- Drinks are served from the right.
- The fork goes on the left side of the plate; the knife and spoon are placed on the right side of the plate. To remember this, "fork" has four letters and "left" has four letters, so the fork goes on the left side of the plate. "Knife" and "spoon" both contain five letters like "right;" therefore, the knife and spoon are placed on the right side.
- Don't apologize for the food you have.

Entertaining Overnight Guests

Just as the Shunammite woman provided all the "comforts of home" for Elisha, we should be considerate of those staying in our home. The Bible says she provided him a little chamber, a bed, a table and stool, and a candlestick (2 Kings 4:10). This is a good starting point for us as well. I would imagine that most preachers would prefer to stay in a hotel versus someone's home. So when one does stay in our home, I try to make his stay as comfortable and private as possible. Consider the following tips when hosting overnight guests:

- If you give up your room and you have small children, encourage your guest to lock the door. We had a visiting pastor and his wife spend the night, but we forgot to tell them to lock the door. We had one toddler who crawled in our bed each night, so on this particular night, we told her we were not sleeping in our room. The next morning, the pastor and his wife walked out holding our daughter. Oops! We never forgot to remind our guests of this again!
- Make sure you have fresh, clean sheets. Iron (with starch) the pillowcases, if you'd like to add a special touch. Fabric softener sheets left between the sheets will give them a fresh scent. There is a spray you can even purchase for freshening linens.
- Extras are nice to have: a table or desk for study, a bowl of fresh fruit, a box of candy, a pitcher and glass of water, tissues, note pad and pen, a single flower, a basket of extra toiletries.
- Give them choices, such as: "Would you like breakfast?" "Would you prefer to take an afternoon nap?"
- Offer to let them use the washer and dryer.

Enjoying Hospitality in Someone Else's Home

When you are enjoying hospitality in someone's home, don't forget to observe the following principles:

- Always be courteous. Don't monopolize the conversation. When you're a guest in their home, never argue or criticize.
- Be appreciative. Say "thank you" and have your kids say "thank you." Notice the special things your hostess has done. Be sure to write a thank you note.

- Offer to help.
- If you are an overnight guest, make the bed, clean the bathroom, and take your dishes to the kitchen. Ask the hostess what would be a help to her. For example, strip the bed, empty the trash, etc.
- Be on time.

Hospitality does not have to be frightening! Missing out on hospitality is missing out on a blessing. I could not begin to tell you how our family has learned to love caring for people and hosting them in our home. Our best friendships, most treasured ministry memories, and most cherished "life-change" stories have often come to us through the times that we have hosted guests in our home.

God works through vulnerability and transparency, and there's no doubt to you or your guests that when you open your home, you are being vulnerable and transparent. In that setting, at least for our ministry, God has done some wonderful things in the lives of people, not the least of which would be our own family.

People often comment about the sweet spirit of the Lancaster Baptist Church family. It is unique. It is hard to find. And I truly believe it is the fruit (at least in part) of the spirit of hospitality that permeates our church. It has truly become the heart of my husband and family to love people with Christ's love through hospitality.

Hospitality—it's a good thing!

CHAPTER FIFTEEN

Being a Blessing to Your Church Family

Ye are our epistle written in our hearts, known and read of all men.—2 CORINTHIANS 3:2

What type of reaction do people have when they hear your name? Do they think "gossip"? Do they sigh and turn away? Or do they smile and think of what a genuine blessing you are? Dorcas was a sincere Christian with an evident heart for God and others. The Bible says that Dorcas was full of good works and almsdeeds, or acts of charity. She was such a blessing during her lifetime that when she died, all of her friends wept and showed the coats that Dorcas had made for them.

> *Now there was at Joppa a certain disciple named Tabitha, which by interpretation is called Dorcas: this woman was full of good works and almsdeeds which she did.*—ACTS 9:36

*Then Peter arose and went with them. When he was come, they
brought him into the upper chamber: and all the widows stood
by him weeping, and shewing the coats and garments which
Dorcas made, while she was with them.*—Acts 9:39

My husband has a plaque that reads, "I want my children
to sorrow my dying, not my living." That is a pretty powerful
thought, isn't it? Of course, we do not want our children, our
husbands, or our church families to sorrow our living more
than our dying. I believe we all want to be a blessing to others—
especially those who are a part of our church families.

I have a dear friend whose sister had a cat to which she was
very strongly attached. One particular weekend she needed a cat-
sitter, so she asked her parents if they would mind watching her
cat. The parents, who did not share her love for cats, reluctantly
agreed.

All seemed to be going well initially, as early the next
morning the mom let the cat outside. But the entire day passed
by before she realized that she had forgotten to let the cat back
in! In somewhat of a panic, she ran to the back door and began
calling the cat. It wasn't long before an obviously half dead cat
appeared at the back door. Feeling terrible for her negligence,
she immediately took the cat to the vet and asked him to save
her daughter's cat. This cat was in pretty bad shape, so the vet
wasn't too hopeful. Nonetheless, that mother paid $400.00 for vet
services that day to spare the life of her daughter's cat.

Some hours later, the vet entered the waiting room to tell the
mother that he had done everything he could to no avail—the cat
was dead. The mother dreaded the thought of telling her daughter
this terrible news.

At this point, the vet offered a complimentary cat burial
ceremony complete with flowers, a grave, and a monthly family
newsletter from the cemetery. The mom thought it was the least
she could do, so she agreed.

When the daughter returned from her trip a few days later, her parents shared what had happened. They were sitting on the back patio trying to comfort their daughter, when surprisingly the daughter's cat suddenly appeared in perfect condition!

It was only then that everyone realized—some stray cat had just had a very nice burial!

There will be times when our efforts to be a blessing are going to cost us more than we realize! Being a blessing takes hard work, determination, and personal sacrifice—and even then, sometimes your efforts will seem to fall short or will go unnoticed. In these pages, I want to challenge you to seize every opportunity you can to serve others and to be a blessing to your church family.

Be a Blessing by Bearing Burdens

You can reach out to your church family by bearing their burdens. God commands us to bear one another's burdens. Galatians 6:2 says, *"Bear ye one another's burdens, and so fulfil the law of Christ."* And John 15:12 tells us, *"This is my commandment, That ye love one another, as I have loved you."*

A burden is defined as "the care we carry in our heart." Everyone carries a burden—everyone. Just look around your church family—young, old, new, and mature Christians—they all carry some burden in their hearts that you can help to bear.

One lady may be praying for a daughter or son to come back to the Lord. Another woman may be praying for the salvation of her husband. Yet another is worried that her marriage is beyond repair.

A teenager may also carry the "weight of the world" on his shoulders as he faces peer pressure, school work, and the struggles of home life. Even a child may carry the burden of a lost relative, abuse, or the pain of a broken home. Tragically, we usually fail to see the burdens others carry.

In November of 1998, we hosted a ladies' retreat in Glendale, California. After one of the services at that retreat, a few of us decided to walk across the street to a corner restaurant for some pie. We were seated at a big table closest to the register, and it wasn't long before we were telling one story after another, laughing until we were crying.

In the middle of our laughter, one of the ladies said "There goes a police officer…." Not thinking much of it, the rest of us just kept talking and laughing. A moment later she said, "There goes another police officer…" and again, we didn't stop to notice what was going on. When she said it the third time, it finally got our attention! We immediately stopped our conversation and looked around. There were police officers everywhere!

While we were sitting there, a thief had entered the restaurant, held up the cashier at gun-point, and took her to the back of the restaurant to pistol whip her. We were oblivious! We completely missed the entire episode! When we were questioned about what happened, the officer couldn't believe that we were less than ten feet away and we didn't see or hear a thing!

Isn't that how we all tend to live our lives? We get so wrapped up in our own enjoyment, our own comfort, and our own agenda that we fail to see the burdens of others. Friend, if you're going to be a blessing to others, it begins with making an effort to see the burdens.

Moses did exactly that in Exodus 2:11, "*And it came to pass in those days, when Moses was grown, that he went out unto his brethren, and looked on their burdens: and he spied an Egyptian smiting an Hebrew, one of his brethren.*"

Just as that waitress did not cry out for help, people carrying heavy burdens often don't cry out for help either. If you're going to bear another's burdens, you will almost always have to be on the lookout for them. You will need to find the burdens, because they most likely won't find you. If you're not searching for them you will probably miss them altogether.

Bear in mind, you're not looking for burdens in an effort to *remove* them—that's usually not God's purpose. God allows burdens to produce spiritual growth, which means we can't always remove them. Yet we *can* strengthen and encourage someone in a time of trial. Phillip Brooks said, "I do not pray for a lighter load, but for a stronger back." He also said, "The truest help we can render an afflicted man is not to take his burden from him, but to call out his best strength that he may be able to bear the burden." Determine to reinforce the Christian rather than remove the burden!

Exodus 17:10–12 gives us this story of two men who bore the burden for Moses. *"So Joshua did as Moses had said to him, and fought with Amalek: and Moses, Aaron, and Hur went up to the top of the hill. And it came to pass, when Moses held up his hand, that Israel prevailed: and when he let down his hand, Amalek prevailed. But Moses' hands were heavy; and they took a stone, and put it under him, and he sat thereon; and Aaron and Hur stayed up his hands, the one on the one side, and the other on the other side; and his hands were steady until the going down of the sun."*

So what do we do for someone with a burden? First, we can uphold her through prayer. Don't just *say* you'll pray, but really *do* it! If you have a short memory, take a minute to pray with her before you forget. You may want to keep a little steno pad in your purse to record prayer requests to go over later. Write a note of encouragement and reassure the discouraged one of your prayers.

> *I exhort therefore, that, first of all, supplications, prayers, intercessions, and giving of thanks, be made for all men; For kings, and for all that are in authority; that we may lead a quiet and peaceable life in all godliness and honesty.*— 1 TIMOTHY 2:1–2

> *Be careful for nothing; but in every thing by prayer and supplication with thanksgiving let your requests be made known unto God.*—PHILIPPIANS 4:6

Cast thy burden upon the LORD, and he shall sustain thee: he shall never suffer the righteous to be moved.—Psalm 55:22

Sharing Scripture is another effective approach to bearing burdens. If you have gone through a similar trial, share a Bible verse that helped you during that time. Be careful of saying, "I know what you're going through." This statement is very seldom true, and it can tend to take away from or minimize what someone is dealing with. Statements like this focus on self more than on the person who is suffering. I have been with many women who attempted to offer comfort, but within minutes, the entire conversation was all about themselves and the trials *they* had experienced. This isn't what a discouraged person needs to hear! She needs to hear the promises of God's Word!

This is good news for those who struggle with "what to say" to a person during a trial. Share God's Word! He promises that His Word will not return void. Isaiah 55:11 says, *"So shall my word be that goeth forth out of my mouth: it shall not return unto me void, but it shall accomplish that which I please, and it shall prosper in the thing whereto I sent it."* It is the Holy Spirit through the power of Scripture Who brings true comfort to the heart of a suffering Christian.

Be a Blessing by Loving Everyone

A Peanuts cartoon portrayed Linus making this statement— "I love mankind. It's people I can't stand." I've heard those who are in ministry tease, "I would love the ministry if it weren't for the people!" Someone else said, "It is no chore for me to love the whole world. My real problem is my neighbor next door!"

Sometimes loving those closest to us is the hardest thing to do. We can give money to feed the poor on the other side of the world, but being kind to those that sit across from our pew? Now that's a different story!

Real love is not a respecter of persons. It's that simple. True love doesn't have an on and off switch. As we grow in God's grace, we will love everyone!

For there is no respect of persons with God.—ROMANS 2:11

Joseph of the Old Testament is an incredible testimony of unconditional and undivided love. Despite his circumstances, he showed love to everyone with whom he came in contact. He loved those who loved him, those who hurt him, and those who were down and out! He loved his family after they sold him into slavery. He loved the prison keeper when he was wrongfully imprisoned. He even reached out to the captain of the guard and to the baker. His love was not partial and was not based on his own circumstances. He decided to love everybody, no matter what was going on in his own life!

You will have these same types of people in your church —those who love you, those who hurt you, and those who are down and out—those whom no one else loves. Friend, if you truly desire to be like Christ, you will be interested in showing love to *everyone* regardless of who she is or where she comes from. You will love the people in all three of these groups.

Love always requires action. It is a choice that demands initiative. While there are many ways to express the love of Christ to others, we must determine to put our love into action. Love is not a warm and fuzzy feeling or a good intention. Love is action! We should be like that telephone commercial that says, "Reach out and touch someone!" The power of a simple act of love cannot be overstated. Little acts of kindness communicate acceptance and love in an amazing way.

In a recent study from UCLA it was found that to simply "maintain emotional and physical health, men and women need eight to ten meaningful touches each day." Think about that. Each person you meet in a given day could use a warm smile, a nice word, or a small gesture of kindness! Even those who have hurt or wounded us need these loving touches. True love will go the extra mile and treat even the most difficult people with genuine consideration.

Let me encourage you to commit yourself to loving and encouraging everybody with whom you come into contact. Be like Joseph. Be patient with people. Listen to them. Say something kind. Offer a compliment. Be the love of Christ personified to those you meet today.

There will also be some actions that you must avoid to love sincerely. Never look down on others or make them feel inferior. Don't be easily angered or hold a grudge. And when others fail, don't give up on them. Our love should not be conditional. It should not be based on performance, but rather on a belief that God creates and values us all just the way we are.

Where does this kind of love come from? Quite simply, it is only possible through prayer and through Spirit-filled living. We cannot attain this kind of love on our own, but the Holy Spirit will bear this love in our lives if we will allow Him to do so!

Evangeline Booth, the daughter of the founder of the Salvation Army, sat in a broken-down slum one day, cleaning the sores of a drunk woman. "I wouldn't do that for a million dollars," said a friend. "Neither would I," replied Ms. Booth. "Our motive for loving people is not money, fame, duty, or acceptance. Our motive must be the love of Christ and the glory of God."

Why should we love everyone? Because God commands us to!

If ye fulfil the royal law according to the scripture, Thou shalt love thy neighbour as thyself, ye do well.—JAMES 2:8

This is my commandment, That ye love one another, as I have loved you.—JOHN 15:12

These things I command you, that ye love one another.—JOHN 15:17

But as touching brotherly love ye need not that I write unto you: for ye yourselves are taught of God to love one another.
—1 THESSALONIANS 4:9

Seeing ye have purified your souls in obeying the truth through the Spirit unto unfeigned love of the brethren, see that ye love one another with a pure heart fervently.—1 Peter 1:22

For this is the message that ye heard from the beginning, that we should love one another.—1 John 3:11

And now I beseech thee, lady, not as though I wrote a new commandment unto thee, but that which we had from the beginning, that we love one another.—2 John 1:5

Not only is "loving one another" a command, it is also a method of expressing the love of Christ to a lost world. We show Christ in our lives by displaying love to the world. John 13:34–35 says, "*A new commandment I give unto you: That ye love one another; as I have loved you, that ye also love one another. By this shall all men know that ye are my disciples, if ye have love one to another.*"

Allow me to share this story with you as you consider the power of showing Christ's love to others:

> Karen and I were the proud "Parents of the Day" at our son, Michael's, kindergarten class. We had fun as he toured us around his classroom and introduced us to all his friends. We joined in for cut and paste, and we spent the better part of the morning in the sandbox. It was a riot!
>
> "Circle up!" called the teacher, "It's story time." Not wanting to look out of place, Karen and I circled up with the rest of our new buddies. After finishing the story entitled "Big," the teacher asked this enthusiastic group, "What makes you feel big?" "Bugs make me feel big," yelled one young student. "Ants," hollered another. "Mosquitoes," called out one more.
>
> The teacher, trying to bring some order back to the class, started calling on children with their hands up. Pointing to one little girl, the teacher said, "Yes dear, what makes you feel big?" "My mommy," was the reply. "How does your mommy make you feel big?" quizzed the teacher. "That's easy," said the child. "When she hugs me and says, 'I love you, Jessica!'"

When we love others, we make them feel "big"—we give them importance and significance. There is someone within your reach today that needs this kind of love, and God expects you to give it to her.

Be a Blessing by Being an Encourager

A young mom was having one of "those days"—the washing machine broke, unexpected bills arrived, the telephone wouldn't stop ringing, and her head ached. She was at her breaking point. She put her toddler in the high chair and then laid her head on the tray and began to cry. Without a word her son took his pacifier out of his mouth and stuck it into hers!

Ever have one of those days? We've all experienced rough situations in which we could have used some encouragement. So have the ladies in your church!

The great thing about being an encouragement is that it's easy. It doesn't have to take a lot of time. It doesn't have to cost a lot, and it doesn't require talent! It only requires a willingness to be used of God and a sensitivity to the leading of the Holy Spirit.

One day, God laid a person on my husband's heart. Not knowing why he felt this particular burden, he asked one of our pastoral staff men to go visit this man to see if we could be a blessing in any way. Later that day, our assistant pastor stopped by the man's home for a visit.

As our assistant pastor began talking, this particular man broke down in tears and confessed that he was going through some very deep trials. He told our assistant pastor that moments before his arrival, he was preparing to take his own life!

This was an unforgettable lesson for all of us on the importance of obeying the Holy Spirit's promptings. If you will listen and respond to God, you'll be surprised who He will lay on your heart and how often you will be compelled to intervene with a gesture of kindness!

As I was writing this chapter this morning, a dear lady of our church with a watchful concern for her pastor's family called to say that the Lord had laid our family on her heart. She stopped by later in the afternoon to drop off a small gift. What a blessing and encouragement she was to me!

"Ministry is always a matter of the heart. If your heart is filled with a watchful concern for God's people, you will be privileged to refresh many souls in need of encouragement just as a rain cloud delivers much needed moisture to a parched earth."

Encouragement goes straight to the heart. In fact, the word itself comes from a combination of the prefix *en* which means "*to put into*" and the Latin word *cor* which means "heart". We literally have the ability to pour hope, strength, and spiritual motivation into the heart of another Christian. That's a pretty awesome privilege!

Being an encouragement is not hard! It's as easy as talking or writing! The Bible encourages us to share positive and encouraging words with others:

> *A man hath joy by the answer of his mouth: and a word spoken in due season, how good is it!*—PROVERBS 15:23

> *Heaviness in the heart of man maketh it stoop: but a good word maketh it glad.*—PROVERBS 12:25

I often keep note cards in my Bible or purse just in case God lays someone on my heart. This enables me to write a quick note, so I won't forget or let an opportunity to be a blessing slip away. I want to be ready to follow the leading of the Holy Spirit as I seek to make a difference in the lives of God's people.

I have a friend who I call "Mrs. Barnabas" because she is such a blessing to me. Among other things, she emails me once a week with a Scripture for the day. We can bless others with Scripture, God's written Word!

Sometimes just being there for a friend will be an encouragement beyond measure. We had some very close

220 It's a Wonderful Life

friends in another state going through an extremely difficult time recently. My husband and I wanted to be an encouragement to them. Almost simultaneously we both said, "We need to be with them." Sometimes you have to get close to comfort and encourage. Remember it is okay to cry—your tears communicate a lot.

Ask the Holy Spirit to guide you, so you know when it's the right time to send a note, to shed a tear, to exhort, to pray, to speak, or just to be there—and obey what He tells you to do.

Encouragement will not only make a person feel better for the moment—it will make a huge, *long-term* difference.

♦   Encouragement will help others to do what's right and to be faithful to God's house. Hebrews 10:24–25 says, *"And let us consider one another to provoke unto love and to good works: Not forsaking the assembling of ourselves together, as the manner of some is; but exhorting one another: and so much the more, as ye see the day approaching."*

♦   Encouragement will help keep those that are weaker in the faith from quitting. Acts 11:22–23 states, *"Then tidings of these things came unto the ears of the church which was in Jerusalem: and they sent forth Barnabas, that he should go as far as Antioch. Who, when he came, and had seen the grace of God, was glad, and exhorted them all, that with purpose of heart they would cleave unto the Lord."*

♦   Encouragement will draw out the potential in others. Deuteronomy 1:37–39 says, *"Also the LORD was angry with me for your sakes, saying, Thou also shalt not go in thither. But Joshua the son of Nun, which standeth before thee, he shall go in thither: encourage him: for he shall cause Israel to inherit it. Moreover your little ones, which ye said should be a prey, and your children, which in that day had no knowledge between good and evil, they shall go in thither, and unto them will I give it, and they shall possess it."*

Sometimes a simple word of encouragement is all it takes to prompt someone to attempt great things for God!

Be a Blessing through Servant Leadership

There are days when I could be very content to stay home, study my Bible all day, pray for long hours, read a book, and simply grow in knowledge! But I don't want to be like a stagnant pond that takes in but never gives out. That's not God's plan for me. First Corinthians 8:1 says, "...*Knowledge puffeth up, but charity edifieth.*" Personal application is one of the reasons God commands me to spend time in His Word! He desires that I would love, serve, and edify others as a result of my time with Him.

We have a saying at Lancaster Baptist Church, "Every member a minister, every saint a servant." We are all called to serve the Lord, regardless of our age or status in life. And, you can't serve God without serving people.

First, we should realize it is the Lord we serve. We see Mary ministering to the body of Christ in John 12:1–3. The church is the body of Christ today. When we minister to the church family, we are doing so as unto the Lord. Serving is not about impressing or gaining the attention of others. Serving is all about our expression of love to the Lord. Colossians 3:23 tells us, "*And whatsoever ye do, do it heartily, as to the Lord, and not unto men.*"

One day, while walking with some children, Queen Mary was caught in a sudden shower. Quickly taking shelter on the porch of a home, she knocked at the door and asked to borrow an umbrella. "I'll send it back tomorrow," she said. The queen had deliberately disguised her appearance by putting on a hat that partly covered her face and by wearing some very plain clothes. The homeowner, reluctant to give a stranger her best umbrella, offered her a castoff she found in the attic. It was broken and there were several holes in it. Apologizing, she turned it over to the monarch, whom she did not recognize.

The next day she had another visitor—a man with a gold braid on his uniform and an envelope in his hand. "The queen sent me with this letter," he said, "and also asked me to thank you personally for the loan of your umbrella." Stunned, the woman burst into tears. "Oh, what an opportunity I missed that I did not give my very best," she cried.

If we knew we were able to serve the queen, we'd give her our best. Yet we *are* serving the King of King*s*, so let's give *Him* our best! Always remember that He is the One Whom we are serving.

Second, we are to serve with gladness and joy. Psalm 100:2 says, *"Serve the LORD with gladness: come before his presence with singing."*

Don't lose your joy in serving. Martha compared herself to Mary and began to complain that Mary was not doing enough. Consequently, Martha lost her joy. You can serve without being Spirit-filled, but you cannot be filled with the Spirit without serving! When you serve in the power of God's Holy Spirit, you will find great joy! That's the fruit that He produces in a life that is yielded to Him.

If you have lost your joy in serving, check your motivation. Why are you doing what you are doing? Why do you serve? Perhaps you are serving for the applause of men or for some other self-gratification. Perhaps your unmet expectations have robbed your joy. When your motives are pure, God will be your true reward and pleasing Him will be your only expectation. Your acts of service will never go unnoticed by the Lord, and true joy in serving comes when our focus remains on God. Do what you do for the pleasure of the King!

Third, serve with your whole heart and strength! Deuteronomy 10:12 says, *"And now, Israel, what doth the LORD thy God require of thee, but to fear the LORD thy God, to walk in all his ways, and to love him, and to serve the LORD thy God with all thy heart and with all thy soul."* Don't serve half-heartedly. Have a good attitude and give your whole effort and heart to the ministry of Jesus Christ—to the wonderful people that God has called you to serve.

There are many ways to serve the ladies in your church family. Offer to baby-sit for a young mom. If you enjoy cooking or baking, take a meal to a family in need. If you know a lady who has been under the weather, volunteer to help with house cleaning or with personal errands. Offer to drive a senior saint to the doctor and sit with her. Volunteer this week to help in the church nursery.

> *Whatsoever thy hand findeth to do, do it with thy might; for there is no work, nor device, nor knowledge, nor wisdom, in the grave, whither thou goest.*—ECCLESIASTES 9:10

> *And whatsoever ye do in word or deed, do all in the name of the Lord Jesus, giving thanks to God and the Father by him.*
> —COLOSSIANS 3:17

An elderly widow, restricted in her activities, was eager to serve Christ. After praying about this, she realized that she could bring blessing to others by playing the piano. The next day she placed this small ad in the *Oakland Tribune*: "Pianist will play hymns by phone daily for those who are sick and despondent—the service is free." The notice included the number to dial.

When people called, she would ask, "What hymn would you like to hear?" Within a few months her playing had brought cheer to several hundred people. Many of them freely poured out their hearts to her, and she was able to help and encourage them.

> Do all the good you can,
> By all the means you can,
> In all the ways you can,
> In all the places you can,
> At all the times you can,
> To all the people you can,
> As long as ever you can.
> —John Wesley

I mentioned earlier that I could be content staying home and just learning. On the flip side, I could also get so involved in serving that I neglect to nurture my relationship with the Lord! Allow me to give you a kind warning: don't get so wrapped up in serving that you no longer have a relationship with the Lord or with your family. The Lord and your family should always be your top priorities. All other ministry service comes after these two priorities.

A. W. Tozer made this observation: "Before the judgment seat of Christ my service will be judged not by how much I have done, but by how much I could have done!"

I have an aunt who has a very expensive set of china. She hardly ever uses it because it cost her so much money. She is afraid it will get chipped or broken. I also have a set china. It is a very inexpensive set, and I use it all the time. If you were to ask me which set is more valuable, I would say mine—because it gets used!

Are you a showcase Christian or a serving Christian? Are you being used or are you afraid to get your hands dirty? I believe our value to God and others increases when we yield ourselves to Him and allow Him to use us for His good pleasure.

Be a Blessing by Being Supportive

If you have ever seen a Colorado Aspen tree, you may have noticed that it does not grow alone. Aspens are found in clusters or groves. The reason is that the Aspen sends up new shoots from the roots. In a small grove, all of the trees may actually be connected at their roots!

Giant California Redwood trees may tower 300 feet into the sky. It would seem that they would require extremely deep roots to anchor them against strong winds. But we're told that their roots are actually quite shallow—in order to capture as much surface water as possible. And they spread in all directions, intertwining with other redwoods. Locked together in this way, all the trees support each other in wind and storms. Like the aspen, they never stand "alone." They need one another to survive. A true church family provides that same type of support. We are connected by a root system that is founded in Christ. Like these trees, we are meant to support one another.

We can support the ladies of our church by being there for the important events of their lives. I believe it's important that you do everything possible to attend showers, weddings, and other special occasions. If you are unable to attend, send a gift with a note, or make a phone call to let them know you care.

It is also vitally important to support the program of the church. Attend ladies' retreats and Bible studies. Actively participate in soulwinning and outreach. It is a blessing to see people faithfully supporting the different ministries of the church. And it's a blessing for people in the church to see you attending and participating as well. A lady in ministry sends a sad message of apathy and spiritual lethargy when she chooses not to be visibly and faithfully involved in the ministries of the church.

I enjoy reading the example of support in Exodus 17:10–12. Israel prevailed when support was given. Our ladies will triumph in Christ as we show our ongoing support for their spiritual growth.

Be a Blessing by Taking Initiative

Someone said there are three types of people in the world: those who do not know what is happening; those who watch what is happening; and those who make things happen. How does this apply to a Christian woman? There are those who do not see a visitor, those who watch the visitor, and those who will reach out to the visitor. This is initiative. Victor Hugo wrote, "Initiative is doing the right things without being told."

Ruth of the Old Testament showed this type of initiative. She didn't have a manual to follow or classes to take. She simply saw opportunities and seized them. She stayed with Naomi, gleaned in the fields, and presented her situation to Boaz. As a result she became the great-grandmother of David. Don't just sit around and watch things happen. Take action to participate in what God wants to accomplish through you! My husband often says, "See the need, and take the lead."

Fear is the number one reason we do not take initiative. We know we should greet the lady who comes to our church for the first time. We know we should invite every lady to attend Bible study or ladies' activities. But the fear of leaving our comfort zones causes us to say nothing. We must remember that fear doesn't come from the Lord, and to be a blessing to others, we must leave our areas of comfort to embrace the courage that God has available for us.

A second enemy of initiative is procrastination. Procrastination is our tendency to postpone. Isn't it easier to do what we enjoy doing instead of what needs to be done?

Procrastination reveals itself through excuses. For example, we say, "I'll call her later," "I'll send that note tomorrow," or "I'll make that visit next week." We are more apt to make excuses when we are self-oriented. If we are truly crucified with Christ, our "excuse-maker" will be out of commission!

When you believe in what you are doing and take the initiative to actually do it—you can make a big difference for the cause of Christ. Here are a couple of ways we can take the initiative:

We should be the first to practice forgiveness. You may have been hurt in the past. If so, you may have a tendency to withdraw or avoid making contact. Romans 12:18 says, *"If it be possible, as much as lieth in you, live peaceably with all men."* "As much as lieth in me" tells me that I need to take the initiative to ensure reconciliation.

We should be the first to initiate hospitality. We should seek out that visitor, invite ladies to an activity, and meet a new member. Don't wait for someone else to be a blessing to you. Leave your comfort zone. Be courageous. Let God use you, but you make the first move. Take initiative.

Be a Blessing by Being a Nurturer

The American Heritage Dictionary defines nurture as "the act of promoting development or growth; upbringing; rearing." We are to nurture and mentor the ladies in our church families to grow closer to God.

Mentoring is very similar to running an Olympic relay race. The older, more experienced leaders who are running the Christian race are in the process of passing the baton to those coming up behind. In an Olympic race, the baton is not suddenly and quickly handed off. The person accepting it may not be ready yet, and it may drop. For a time, the experienced runner allows the upcoming runner to run alongside him until they are both ready. Mentoring is running alongside someone else for as long as it takes. Who are you running alongside at the moment?

You may not feel qualified to be a mentor. You may not feel that you have the ability to teach or train. But this is all beside the point! The fact is—if you are a Christian, God intends for you to grow in maturity to the point that you can nurture someone else in the Christian life. He will give you wisdom and discernment. He will enable you, and He will equip you. You must make the choice.

The Bible has much to say on the subject of mentoring others. Notice how it is not only suggested, but it is commanded in 1 Timothy 4:12–16:

> *Let no man despise thy youth; but be thou an example of the believers, in word, in conversation, in charity, in spirit, in faith, in purity. Till I come, give attendance to reading, to exhortation, to doctrine. Neglect not the gift that is in thee, which was given thee by prophecy, with the laying on of the hands of the presbytery. Meditate upon these things; give thyself wholly to them; that thy profiting may appear to all. Take heed unto thyself, and unto the doctrine; continue in them: for in doing this thou shalt both save thyself, and them that hear thee.*

Mentoring is a spiritual commitment to develop spiritual excellence in another. We can show this commitment to those in our church by applying these characteristics:

- **Be available.** Ladies need to feel as if they are not inconveniencing you.
- **Be trustworthy.** Others you are mentoring must be able to trust you implicitly.
- **Be flexible and God-honoring.** Remember, your ultimate goal is to point them to Christ. "If I slip into the place that can be filled by Christ alone, making myself the first necessity to a soul instead of leading it to fasten upon Him, then I know nothing of Calvary's love" (Amy Carmichael).

Always remember your commitment to help a people reach their full potential for Christ. Paul said it this way in 2 Timothy 2:2, *"And the things that thou hast heard of me among many witnesses, the same commit thou to faithful men, who shall be able to teach others also."* Start by asking God to give you a desire to mentor newborn or younger Christians. You may begin mentoring simply by explaining how to have a meaningful and personal relationship with Christ. You may ask them to be your soulwinning partner, and train them by example.

Mentoring requires a personal approach. My husband has said so often, "No one cares how much you know, until they know how much you care." Do your people know how much you care? Commit to a personal ministry approach and allow God to use you in the lives of others.

Be a Blessing by Being Genuine

I heard the story of a brand-new lawyer in his brand-new office on his first day in practice. As a prospective client walked in the door he decided he should look busy and important. So he picked up the phone and started talking: "Look, Harry, about that merger deal. I think I better run down to the factory and handle it personally. Yes. No. I don't think three million will swing it. We'd better have Rogers from Seattle meet us there. Okay. Call you back later." Hanging up the phone, he looked up at the potential client and said, "Good morning, how may I help you?" To which the man at the door replied, "You can't help me at all. I'm just here to hook up your phone."

One of the strongest words spoken by Jesus while He was on this earth was the word "hypocrite." He lumps hypocrites right in there with the scribes and Pharisees. Matthew 23:14 says, "*Woe unto you, scribes and Pharisees, hypocrites! for ye devour widows' houses, and for a pretence make long prayer: therefore ye shall receive the greater damnation.*"

None of us will be perfect until we get to Heaven, and until then, God expects us to be genuine! I heard a preacher once say, "You will always come in second place if you try to be something or someone you are not. If you just be who God made you, you will come in first every time."

Each of us is a work in progress. You do not have to reach a certain plateau of the "ultimate Christian woman" or "the ultimate pastor's wife" to count your life a success. If that were the case, my singing ability and piano skills would put me out of that contest altogether! It's not my ability or talent that allows me to be in the ministry—it's the call of God. And it's not my ability that makes me effective in the ministry—it's the power of God. I can get on with serving God as the person He created me to be, or I can waste my life trying to be someone that I'm not! I choose to be who God created me to be, and to live my life today as He intends. If God has a specific plan made just for me to fulfill, why would I want to be anybody else?

"Half of the misery in the world comes from trying to look, instead of trying to be, what one is not!" (George McDonald). Be the woman God wants you to be. People will more easily relate to a woman that is real and down-to-earth than a woman who is putting on a show—and both are usually obvious! Anne of Green

Gables called it "putting on airs." We are not playing a part! God tells us to be holy, but He doesn't tell us to be "holier than thou."

When a man wants to buy a woman a diamond ring, the first decision he is going to make is if it will be a real diamond or a cubic zirconium. Now, we all know what the woman would prefer. We would prefer the diamond because it is real and worth more. Those around you would prefer the real you, too, because you are worth more that way!

We have a great opportunity to be a blessing to those that God has placed in our church. Everyone needs a little encouragement! Everyone is special in God's eyes and deserves to be treated that way.

I love the story of one little boy who said to his father: "Let's play darts. I'll throw, and you say 'Wonderful!'" He longed for the support of his father!

William Arthur Ward said, "Flatter me, and I may not believe you. Criticize me, and I may not like you. Ignore me, and I may not forgive you. Encourage me, and I will not forget you." When it's within our power to do so, let's endeavor to be the blessing and encouragement God wants us to be!

CHAPTER SIXTEEN

Challenges in the Ministry

eloved, think it not strange concerning the fiery trial which is to try you, as though some strange thing happened unto you.—1 Peter 4:12

The way to Heaven is ascending; we must be content to travel up hill, though it be hard and tiresome, and contrary to the natural bias of our flesh.—Jonathan Edwards

Several years ago, we took a vacation to Maui. Upon arriving in Hawaii, we sat down as a family and discussed what we wanted to do and see while we were there. We had all heard about the Road to Hana, known as the "Highway to Heaven." It sounded like an adventurous road, so we decided to experience it firsthand. We were all excited to take the journey as we loaded into the van and headed for the town of Hana that next morning.

The Road to Hana is probably one of the most beautifully breathtaking and scenic roads in the world. But it is not without some bumps in the road—well, actually curves in the road! This highway is made up of about fifty-two miles of undeveloped road, many, many feet above the water. You must keep your eyes on the road at all times! The infamous road has 617 curves, or over ten switchback curves per mile! You cross over fifty-six very old, one-lane bridges as you journey to the top. There are no restaurants, no gas stations, and no bathrooms along the way, and it takes about four hours (one way) to reach your destination! The trip is not for the faint of heart.

Not too long into our journey, we began to see people scattered along the side of the road. They weren't stopping to enjoy the scenery. They were getting sick! We all commented, "Those poor people..." as we passed by. Little did we know that a few hours later it would be *our* car along the side of the road and my husband would be the one who was getting sick (and he was the driver!).

Though the road was challenging, it was a drive of a lifetime! Some of our family's best memories were made on that trip. I am glad we stuck it out to the end.

We are all on the road of life! And I'm sure that, like me, you have experienced God's blessing along the way! In our twenty- five years of ministry, we have enjoyed seeing people saved and watching God bless our church. We have been part of many miracles. Serving the Lord is an awesome journey!

Though the journey is incredible, it is not without challenges. The challenges that Christian workers face today are hard and many. Our family and ministry have faced difficulties in many various forms over the years.

We have experienced *disappointments*. My husband often says, "People are never where you think they are." There are those with whom we have invested time, shared Scripture, encouraged, prayed for, and wept with, only to see them quit on the Lord, like Diotrephes of the New Testament. It can be greatly disappointing when this takes place.

We have also endured *health issues.* In 1990, I ruptured two discs in my back and was hospitalized and bedridden for several weeks. It wasn't easy trying to manage the home from a bed! That situation was one of those challenging experiences for our family.

Several of our church members have experienced serious health problems. We have hurt *with* them. It is not easy to see church members battling long and serious illnesses. In 2000, one of our young staff wives, Lori Thomasson, died of cancer. Though she possessed the joy of the Lord throughout her final days on earth, it was difficult to see her suffer physically.

We have gone through *tragedies.* Several years ago, Jessica, one of our college-age church members, was in a car accident while leaving our church campus. She wasn't expected to live and was in a coma for quite some time. Our entire church family felt the pain and rallied together in prayer for her life. It was physically and emotionally exhausting for many of us. (We praise the Lord that God answered those prayers and healed Jessica.)

On more than one occasion we have been the object of *criticism.* I heard someone say once, "Criticism is as inevitable as ants at a picnic."

Criticism *is* inevitable! When you experience it, don't let it hinder your service to God! An initial response to criticism may be to stop what you are doing. For instance, if my husband criticizes the way I iron his shirt, I could respond, "Fine! From now on you can iron your own shirts, because I'm not doing it anymore!" That response may be the one I *want* to give, but it is definitely not the right thing to do or say! If you have been criticized and are tempted to question or give up on the purpose of God in your ministry, please remember: "Never doubt in the night, what God has given in the light."

I am often reminded of a familiar story in the Bible. After a great victory (have you ever noticed that most of the trials, criticism, problems, and discouragement come after a great victory?), wicked Queen Jezebel was after the prophet, Elijah. She wanted him to be put to death. Instead of focusing on the recently displayed power of God and drawing strength from it, Elijah fled! He ran at the first sign of opposition. We find him sitting under a juniper tree, depressed and ready to die. He quit! (I think Elijah knew that it was wrong to quit on God, so he probably decided that if God would let him die, it would justify his quitting.) Don't be like Elijah! Don't throw in the towel just because someone doesn't appreciate or like what you are doing!

We have dealt with some *difficult people*. When Danielle was fifteen-years-old, a man twice her age began stalking her. He had noticed her in the choir and followed her everywhere she went. Even after being confronted, this man still insisted on wanting to date her. The police finally had to intervene, and the man was not able to come near her again.

On more than one occasion, we have had *death threats* come through our fax machine. One Sunday evening, I immediately knew something was wrong when my husband walked out onto the platform. I noticed a few minutes later that several of our deacons were sitting near our pew. We were rushed home the minute church was over, and it wasn't until we walked in the door that I was made aware of what was going on. One of the men of our church read a fax to me. There was a death threat to "Matthew." I can't begin to tell you the emotion I was feeling. Our Matthew was just a little boy at the time. It was one of the longest nights of my life. After further investigation the next morning, we discovered that the threat was not to *our* "Matthew." The fax was generated from a pro-homosexual group, angry at Christians and churches.

My husband was preaching in northern California when a death threat from a Muslim group was again sent through the fax machine. The threat was immediately given to one of our church members for professional assessment.

While this man was on his way to church, he drove by our home and noticed our front door was wide open. He thought that was strange, so he stopped to check it out. As he looked in the front door he saw trash strewn all over the floor. He took out his gun and began checking the rest of the house. When he turned the corner, he saw the perpetrator, who came very close to losing his life that day. Our family would have been very sad because it was our dog!

The wind was blowing quite hard that morning, and when we left for school, the last one out the front door did not use the dead bolt. The wind was able to blow the door open! Our dog probably thought, "Hey! This is great, my owners never let me in the house!" So he went into the house, and in an effort to find food, spread the trash all over the floor. After his little escapade, he took a nap on the living room floor where he almost was shot to death.

In both of those instances, I am very glad nothing serious came about as a result of the threats. Threats still come, and we continue to evaluate each one. We know that we are ultimately in the Lord's hands.

At other times we have experienced picketers, loneliness, fatigue, and unkind and untruthful accusations against my husband and our children. These forms of gossip and slander are probably the most common and the hardest challenges for me to handle.

I heard someone say, "Gossip has no commitment either to accuracy or good taste." People can be very harsh, cruel, and untruthful in what they say. In fact, the way they give out the information, you would think it was documented testimony!

Criticism is a trial I was not expecting to deal with when we entered the ministry over twenty-five years ago. This has been the one area of difficulty that has surprised me the most. Now, I don't like when people attack me, but it hurts more when they attack my husband or my children. (I guess that's when the mama bear comes out in me!) I know my husband and children better than anyone else, and, though I realize no one is perfect, I do see their consistent desire to walk with the Lord and live for Him. I watch my husband pray for his attackers and care for those who hate him. So, when people attack his integrity or approachability, I really have to give it to the Lord!

When someone makes wounding remarks or when comments about you or your family are vicious and cruel, remember it is a reflection of what is going on inside that person's heart. It's not about you. Those comments are based on emotions and paradigm. You are just the target for the moment.

One day, a man's donkey fell into a well. The animal cried for several hours while the farmer tried to figure out what to do. He finally decided that since the donkey was old and since the well needed to be covered up anyway, it just wasn't worth it to rescue the animal. So he invited all his neighbors to help him cover the well. They all grabbed shovels and began to shovel dirt into the well. At first, the donkey realized what was happening and cried terribly! Then, he quieted down. A few shovel loads later, the farmer looked down the well and was astonished at what he saw. With every shovel of dirt that hit his back, the donkey would shake it off and take a step up. As the neighbors continued to shovel dirt on top of the animal, he would continue to shake it off and take a step up. Pretty soon, the donkey was able to step over the edge of the well!

When people gossip, it's like getting dirt shoveled all over you. It's easy to feel like you are alone in a hole, with no way of escape. But, there is a way out: Shake off the criticism and take a step up!

It is hard to understand what takes place when someone who promises his love, gratitude, and commitment turns his back on you and God with ridicule and slander. In situations like this, we must claim Psalm 147:5 once again, *"Great is our Lord, and of great power: his **understanding is infinite**."* God understands it all, including your broken heart. Trust Him—His sovereignty, His understanding, and His greatness.

The Presence of Trials

We all would choose sunshine over showers, but just imagine what our world would be like if it never rained again! Franklin Elmer described a place of no rain located in Northern Chile. He wrote, "Morning after morning the sun rises brilliantly over the tall mountains to the east; each noon it shines brightly down from overhead; evening brings a picturesque sunset. Although storms are often seen raging high in the mountains, and heavy fog banks are observed far out over the sea, the sun continues to shine on this favored and protected strip of land. One would imagine this area to be an earthly paradise, but it is not. Instead, it is a sterile and desolate desert! There are no streams of water, and nothing grows there." Nothing will grow in a life free of trials. And a life without "rain" does not exist. Here are the facts:

Expect trials to come. I heard a story about a preacher who was walking along a sidewalk one day when he realized he wasn't aware of any trial or persecution in his life. He immediately fell to his knees and asked the Lord if there was sin in his life that he hadn't confessed or if he was being disobedient in an area of his life. Just then, a tenant from up above threw out a milk bottle that hit the preacher right on the head. He said, "Thank you Lord. I was beginning to worry!"

It's been said that there is nothing certain in life but death and taxes. Well, I think we can add trials to that list! Christians *will* experience them!

> Beloved, think it not strange concerning the fiery trial which is
> to try you, as though some strange thing happened unto you.
> —1 PETER 4:12

Trials are burdensome. Even though we know we will experience trials, it is not always easy to accept them. They can be difficult and painful to bear. We may ask God to remove the burden, and, though God may not always take it away, He will give us a stronger shoulder! Corrie Ten Boom said, "If God sends us on stony paths, He provides strong shoes."

In our human minds, it seems that other people's trials are so much easier to bear than our own. There is an old fable that tells of a little village of people who were experiencing trials. They all began to complain, so someone came up with a solution: This town had a special tree located in the center of the village. The people were instructed to write down a trial that was too hard for them to carry and post their paper to the tree. After they all placed their trials on the tree, they were told to go to the tree and pick a trial they thought they *could* handle. Each person picked the trial they had originally written down. And the moral to the story is: God knows exactly what we can handle, and it is not wise or conducive to your spiritual growth to compare your trials with others!

Have you ever noticed the sticker on a liquid medicine bottle that says, "Shake well before using"? That is what God has to do with some of His children. He has to shake them well before they are used. It doesn't always feel pleasant, but it is necessary for effectiveness.

Trials are temporary. We can rejoice in the fact that trials don't last forever (Even though it may seem like they do)! I love Romans 8:18 which says, *"For I reckon that the sufferings of this present time are not worthy to be compared with the glory which shall be revealed in us."* The suffering we temporarily experience on this earth is not even *worthy* to be compared to what God has in store for us in heaven! What a blessed promise to claim for our lives! This life is a temporal life, so keep your heart focused on eternity.

When God allows His children to go through the fire, He keeps His eye on the clock and His hand on the thermostat. He will not allow the fire to get one degree too hot. And He will not permit us to suffer one minute too long. The longest any trial could last is the duration of a lifetime, which in comparison to eternity, is almost nothing! Live with eternity in mind!

Every trial is Father-filtered. Trials are sometimes like medicine, it is easier to take when you know it is good for you. God is a good Father, and He will allow nothing to happen in your life unless it is for your ultimate good.

We see throughout the book of Job how Satan brought trials into Job's life. Each trial was permitted by the Lord, and Satan was limited to what God allowed.

> *There hath no temptation taken you but such as is common to man: but God is faithful, who will not suffer you to be tempted above that ye are able; but will with the temptation also make a way to escape, that ye may be able to bear it.*—1 CORINTHIANS 10:13

Remember: whenever there is the presence of trials, there is the presence of God. Isaiah 43:2 promises, "*When thou passest through the waters, I will be with thee; and through the rivers, they shall not overflow thee: when thou walkest through the fire, thou shalt not be burned; neither shall the flame kindle upon thee.*"

> *God is our refuge and strength, a very present help in trouble.*
> —PSALM 46:1

The Purpose of Trials

Your understanding of God's purpose in testing will determine your ability to withstand the turmoil and uproar that takes place during that testing. Understanding God's purposes will help you to find peace and stability when you are feeling that your world is turned upside down. Trials do have a purpose!

Trials are prescribed to meet our needs. First Peter 1:6 says, "*Wherein ye greatly rejoice, though now for a season, if need be, ye are in heaviness through manifold temptations.*" "If need be" indicates that God knows there will be periods of life in which we need to experience testing. Of course, at the time, we don't think we need the trial, but my kids didn't think they needed to go to school when they were in first grade either! Our Father knows our needs better than we know our own.

Many years ago a woman was traveling with her baby on a stage coach in western Montana. The weather was bitter and cold, and the driver could do nothing to protect her from the elements. He soon noticed that the mother was becoming unconscious from the cold. So he stopped the coach, took the baby, and wrapping it warmly, put it under the seat. He then took the mother by the arm, and dragged her out on the ground. He drove away, leaving her in the road. When she saw him drive away, she ran after him, crying for her baby. When the driver felt sure that she was warm, he slowed the coach and helped her resume her place by her baby.

What at first seemed cruel and difficult for the mother, turned out to be the very thing she needed to save her life. I imagine she was extremely thankful for the trial she endured. The Lord knows when we need a trial and when we need to be shaken up to avoid spiritual death. I hope you are not going through a trial right now—unless you need to be for the sake of your spiritual life. If that is the case, then I pray that you will learn the lessons God has in store for you as a result of this time.

Trials are the pathway back to God. Why is it when things are going well, we have a propensity to go our own way, spend less time on our knees, and seek the Lord with less than our whole heart? Trials are often designed for the purpose of bringing us back to God.

> Before I was afflicted I went astray: but now have I kept thy word.—PSALM 119:67

Trials prove our sincerity. Just as the assayer tests gold to see if it is pure or counterfeit, trials test the sincerity of our faith. A person who abandons his faith when the going gets tough proves that he did not have a genuine faith at all.

Trials prepare us for spiritual growth. The Bible is our Textbook for spiritual growth. Yet most of our growing takes place *outside* the classroom. It is experienced in the circumstances of life. God uses trials to mature us and prepare us for greater usefulness in the future. Someone said, "God may lead us through a trial at age thirty so we can handle a hurricane at age sixty!"

A trial not only tests our faith, it stretches it as well. Testing enables us to grow beyond our original capacity and allows us to attain greater heights in the Lord's work.

When you experience a trying time in your life, remember that God is more interested in your character than your comfort. He wants to perfect you, not pamper you. He wants you to grow spiritually!

> *And he said unto me, My grace is sufficient for thee: for my strength is made perfect in weakness. Most gladly therefore will I rather glory in my infirmities, that the power of Christ may rest upon me.*—2 CORINTHIANS 12:9

Trials purify us. It is God's desire that we would be pure vessels, fit for the Master's use. No one wants to use a dirty cup!

There are times in life when God must not only clean us, but He must mold, bend, hammer, and shape us. These times are difficult to experience, but they are necessary for our purification.

A goldsmith would never deliberately waste precious ore. Instead, he would put it into the furnace long enough to remove the cheap impurities. He would pour it out and make from it a beautiful article of value.

I love how F.B. Meyer describes this process of purification:

> A bar of iron worth $2.50, when wrought into horseshoes is worth $5. If made into needles it is worth $175. If made into penknife blades it is worth $1,625. If made into springs for watches it is worth $125,000. What a "trial by fire" that bar must undergo to be worth this! But the more it is manipulated, and the more it is hammered and passed through the heat, beaten, pounded, and polished—the greater its value.

Christian, are you wondering about the trials through which you are passing? With impatient heart are you saying, "How long, O Lord?" The heat of the flame and the blows of the hammer are necessary if you are to be more than an unpolished, rough bar of iron. God's all-wise plan, though it calls for the fire, produces the valuable watch spring of maturity. His very best for your life has behind it His perfect timing.

For they verily for a few days chastened us after their own pleasure; but he for our profit, that we might be partakers of his holiness.—Hebrews 12:10

Take away the dross from the silver, and there shall come forth a vessel for the finer.—Proverbs 25:4

Trials teach us to personify Christ. Just as the goldsmith keeps the metal in the furnace until he can see his reflection, so our Lord keeps us in the furnace of suffering until we reflect the glory and beauty of Jesus Christ.

Responding to times of difficulty in a Christ-like manner is a great testimony to unsaved people who watch you. As we allow God's grace to work in our hearts, we can also encourage fellow Christians by our faithfulness and example.

Is there no other way open, God except
Through sorrow, pain, and loss,
To stamp Christ's likeness on my soul
No other way except the cross?

Trials point others to God. Many biblical examples prove this principle. The Gospel was spread because of the trial that Paul experienced in the Philippian jail. And because of the persecution of the three Hebrew children, Nebuchadnezzar made a decree that he would destroy those who said anything against the God of Shadrach, Meshach, and Abednego.

Is your response to trials one that can point others to the Saviour? God *will* point all men to Himself. Are you an instrument that He can use to accomplish that purpose?

Trials display the power of God in our lives. I don't know about you, but I need and want God's power in my life! One way to experience God's power is through the presence of trials. God's power is greater than our emotions and our weaknesses, and it is displayed as we allow Him to work in our lives during times of suffering.

Someone once said, "Trials remind us of who we are and who God is." God is an all-powerful God, and He longs to show Himself strong on behalf of those who truly seek to honor Him.

> *And lest I should be exalted above measure through the abundance of the revelations, there was given to me a thorn in the flesh, the messenger of Satan to buffet me, lest I should be exalted above measure. For this thing I besought the Lord thrice, that it might depart from me. And he said unto me, My grace is sufficient for thee: for my strength is made perfect in weakness. Most gladly therefore will I rather glory in my infirmities, that the power of Christ may rest upon me. Therefore I take pleasure in infirmities, in reproaches, in necessities, in persecutions, in distresses for Christ's sake: for when I am weak, then am I strong.*—2 Corinthians 12:7–10

The Lord has more need of our weakness than of our strength. Our strength is often His rival; our weakness is His servant, drawing on His resources, and showing forth His glory. Man's extremity is God's opportunity; man's security is Satan's opportunity. God's way is not to take His children out of a trial, but to give them strength to bear it.

Responding to Trials

Learn from our trials. What is God trying to teach you through this trial? Every trial gives us the opportunity to learn something wonderful about our Saviour. During one trial, we might learn of His grace. The next testing may encourage us with a new awareness of His strength. And the following trial may remind us of His promises and His comfort.

We can also learn to experience and exhibit the fruit of the Spirit: love, joy, peace, longsuffering, gentleness, goodness, faith, meekness, and temperance. Listening and learning rather than being defensive and close-minded is the best way to deal with a difficult situation.

Respond to the trial with God's perspective. Does your trial reveal any areas of your life that need change? If so, confess the sin and get rid of the hindrances.

Perhaps you are being criticized. Consider the accuracy of the criticism. Is there any part that is true? What can you change for God's glory? All leaders get criticized. It's their response to criticism that sets them apart. Our response to trials or to criticism should be different from the world. We should respond like Christ.

If you determine that you brought the trial into your life through sin, irresponsible behavior, or a bad decision, confess it to God. After your confession, take the appropriate steps to resolve it.

If, to your knowledge, you have done nothing to bring the trial upon yourself, assume it is from God's loving hand for your benefit and His glory. Respond by applying the principles taught in the Scripture concerning trials.

Stay faithful. God requires us to be faithful even during tough times. The children of Israel didn't do this. Upon leaving Egypt and experiencing their first trial, they whined and wanted to return to slavery.

The writer of Hebrews says: *"Wherefore seeing we also are compassed about with so great a cloud of witnesses, let us lay aside every weight, and the sin which doth so easily beset us, and let us run with patience the race that is set before us"* (Hebrews 12:1). That means: Don't give out. Don't give in. Don't give up. Don't quit.

Don't jump off the Potter's wheel before the potter is finished molding you into a usable vessel! Finish your course so you can say as Paul did in 2 Timothy 4:7, *"I have fought a good fight, I have finished my course, I have kept the faith."*

To escape a trial could mean to escape God. There is one thing worse than God dealing with you, and that is God *not* dealing with you. So stay faithful.

Encourage yourself in the Lord. My entire family was running late one school day. Matthew seemed to be ready first, so I asked him if he would help make his lunch. Before we left the house, I thought I should check to make sure it contained something healthy! When I looked into his bag, I saw a piece of paper. He had written himself a note and put it in his lunch—just like I would do for him. Matthew knew how to encourage himself!

We see in 1 Samuel how David was "greatly distressed," but he encouraged himself in the Lord. David's faith supplied him with resources for comfort. We should encourage ourselves in the Bible, as well!

> *Hold up my goings in thy paths, that my footsteps slip not. I have called upon thee, for thou wilt hear me, O God: incline thine ear unto me, and hear my speech. Shew thy marvellous lovingkindness, O thou that savest by thy right hand them which put their trust in thee from those that rise up against them. Keep me as the apple of the eye, hide me under the shadow of thy wings.*—PSALM 17:5–8

> *My voice shalt thou hear in the morning, O LORD; in the morning will I direct my prayer unto thee, and will look up.*
> —PSALM 5:3

> *Cast thy burden upon the LORD, and he shall sustain thee: he shall never suffer the righteous to be moved.*—PSALM 55:22

> *Therefore, my beloved brethren, be ye stedfast, unmoveable, always abounding in the work of the Lord, forasmuch as ye know that your labour is not in vain in the Lord.*
> —1 CORINTHIANS 15:58

Not that I speak in respect of want: for I have learned, in whatsoever state I am, therewith to be content.—Philippians 4:11

Many are the afflictions of the righteous: but the LORD delivereth him out of them all.—Psalm 34:19

I press toward the mark for the prize of the high calling of God in Christ Jesus.—Philippians 3:14

Only take heed to thyself, and keep thy soul diligently, lest thou forget the things which thine eyes have seen, and lest they depart from thy heart all the days of thy life: but teach them thy sons, and thy sons' sons.—Deuteronomy 4:9

I have glorified thee on the earth: I have finished the work which thou gavest me to do.—John 17:4

I have fought a good fight, I have finished my course, I have kept the faith.—2 Timothy 4:7

God's Word
To the weary pilgrim, I am a good staff.
To the one who sits in gloom, I am a glorious light.
To those who stoop beneath heavy burdens, I am sweet rest.
To him who has lost his way, I am a safe guide.
To those who are distressed by the storms of life, I am
      an anchor.
To those who suffer in lonely solitude, I am a cool, soft
      hand resting on a fevered brow.
O, child of man, to best defend me, just use me!

Pray. We have covered much on prayer, but the Lord tells us we should pray when we are "afflicted."

Is any among you afflicted? let him pray. Is any merry? let him sing psalms.—James 5:13

Take your trials and burdens to the Lord in prayer; give Him the hurt that is in your heart. I don't know about you, but I have favorite verses and favorite songs for different stages, occasions, or circumstances in my life. My favorite hymn during a time of trial is *What a Friend We Have in Jesus*! It reminds me to pray to my true and faithful Friend, the Lord Jesus.

> What a friend we have in Jesus,
> All our sins and griefs to bear!
> What a privilege to carry
> Everything to God in prayer!
> O what peace we often forfeit,
> O what needless pain we bear,
> All because we do not carry
> Everything to God in prayer.
>
> Have we trials and temptations?
> Is there trouble anywhere?
> We should never be discouraged;
> Take it to the Lord in prayer.
> Can we find a friend so faithful
> Who will all our sorrows share?
> Jesus knows our every weakness;
> Take it to the Lord in prayer.

Don't seek to get even. Let God take care of those that seek to hurt you. He will do a much better job than you will!

But the LORD is my defence; and my God is the rock of my refuge.—PSALM 94:22

The LORD is on my side; I will not fear: what can man do unto me?—PSALM 118:6

Say not thou, I will recompense evil; but wait on the LORD, and he shall save thee.—PROVERBS 20:22

Say not, I will do so to him as he hath done to me: I will render to the man according to his work.—PROVERBS 24:29

Recompense to no man evil for evil. Provide things honest in the sight of all men. If it be possible, as much as lieth in you, live peaceably with all men. Dearly beloved, avenge not yourselves, but rather give place unto wrath: for it is written, Vengeance is mine; I will repay, saith the Lord.—Romans 12:17–19

Say to them, that are of a fearful heart, Be strong, fear not: behold, your God will come with vengeance, even God with a recompence; he will come and save you.—Isaiah 35:4

Rejoice. James 1:2 says, *"My brethren, count it all joy when ye fall into divers temptations."* Unlike happiness, which is dependent upon circumstances, joy is a condition of the heart that we can possess no matter what we are going through.

Joy is a choice! We can choose to pout and feel sorry for ourselves, or we can say, "Okay. God wants my attention here, and I'm glad He's working in my life." When things are going well, we talk about how good God is, and we rejoice in the great things He has done. But what about when the pressures come, the burdens are heavy, and the trials are tough; do we rejoice in the Lord then? Philippians 4:4 tells us, *"Rejoice in the Lord alway: and again I say, Rejoice."*

Because of verses like Psalm 5:11, I can rejoice in the fact that the Lord will defend me from those who are against me: *"But let all those that put their trust in thee rejoice: let them ever shout for joy, because thou defendest them: let them also that love thy name be joyful in thee."*

God promises to meet us when we rejoice in Him. Isaiah 64:5 says, *"Thou meetest him that rejoiceth and worketh righteousness, those that remember thee in thy ways: behold, thou art wroth; for we have sinned: in those is continuance, and we shall be saved."*

God also promises that His joy will sustain us. Nehemiah 8:10 tells us, *"…the joy of the Lord is your strength."* Do you need strength during your trial? Learn to find your joy in the Lord!

Corrie Ten Boom, the well-known Dutch watchmaker who helped to hide Jews in her house during the Holocaust in Europe, was arrested and sent to a Nazi concentration camp. She, too, found it hard to find anything good about her desperate situation.

But her sister Betsie found a hidden blessing. She thanked God for the fleas that tormented them each day. Fleas? Miserable fleas? Yes. The imprisoned women discovered that the presence of the fleas kept the guards away from their barracks, allowing the women to speak freely. It was a blessing wrapped up in a hardship.

Trust. Not too long ago I spent three of four days traveling with my husband on an airplane. Flying terrifies me! I don't know how such a huge, heavy piece of metal can stay up in the air like that! I was amazed at the complete trust displayed by over one hundred passengers boarding that plane! We do not get to meet the pilot until we are 10,000 feet in the air. We do not know if the mechanics did their job correctly. We cannot see the air traffic controllers who are continually making split second decisions to keep planes from colliding. We literally trust our lives to those who build, fly, and direct the plane. Even after bad flying experiences (and I have had a few), we still choose to fly—and we pay for this experience!

Why is it that, as Christians, we can easily trust other humans, but fail to trust the Lord completely when life has a little turbulence?

Sometimes it is hard to trust the Lord through difficult circumstances because we want *our* will or *our* outcome. Trust is allowing *God* to control the circumstances. Fear hinders us from trusting God, because we fret over what might happen or how things will turn out. Remember, God never makes a mistake; He never forgets about us; He never forsakes us; and He will never betray us! You don't have to fear the future! You must simply trust the heart of God.

> For I know the thoughts that I think toward you, saith the LORD, thoughts of peace, and not of evil, to give you an expected end.
> —JEREMIAH 29:11

> And we know that all things work together for good to them that love God, to them who are the called according to his purpose.
> —ROMANS 8:28

Casting all your care upon him; for he careth for you.
—1 PETER 5:7

Wherefore let them that suffer according to the will of God commit the keeping of their souls to him in well doing, as unto a faithful Creator.—1 PETER 4:19

Thou wilt keep him in perfect peace, whose mind is stayed on thee: because he trusteth in thee.—ISAIAH 26:3

> I can't say that I am glad when storm clouds come,
> When days and nights are burdensome and long.
> I like the peacefulness of sunny days
> When life is bright and in my heart's a song.
>
> And yet...I know the wisdom I have learned
> Or any courage that my life displays
> Was never gained in gold sunlit hours
> But rather grew from dark and stormy days.
>
> I've felt God's presence closer 'mid the storm
> as I relied on Him to guide my way
> And through my trials found a stronger faith
> Enabling me to better face each day.
>
> And so, I would not ask God NOT to send
> Those testings fashioned by His loving hand;
> For ALL things work together for my good
> And things once questioned...now I understand.
> —Beverly J. Anderson

Don't become bitter. Trials should make you better, not bitter! A bitter spirit is extremely destructive. It drives wedges between friends, co-laborers, husbands and wives, brothers and sisters, and parents and children. Be ready to rebuild broken relationships that may come as a part of a trial. Always be sensitive to the Spirit's leading toward healing the breach.

Focus on the Lord. When suffering or trials come along, there is a tendency to focus on the pain and the problems.

My little brother was playing in the garage when he was about five-years-old. He wanted to cut a piece of string, but he couldn't find any scissors. So he used a hatchet that was nearby! He missed the string and cut the tips of two fingers! He came running into the house holding his hand. When I saw his two fingers, I wanted to scream, cry, or hide, but my mom told me I had to keep his mind off of his hand. So all the way to the doctor I talked to him about fishing and baseball in an effort to keep his focus away from his pain.

When you are in pain, don't focus on it! Don't examine the wound and rehearse the injury! Focus on God!

If you have had a natural childbirth you were probably taught to have a focal point during labor. The focal point is an article or a location in the room that you look at to take your mind off the painful contractions. The item is also used to encourage you during labor. The focal point can be anything you choose. You can bring a picture of your husband or a baby, or even an item like a teddy bear. The concept is to focus on something positive and encouraging to distract your attention away from the pain.

God must be your focal point when the pain becomes intense! He will provide the encouragement, motivation, and strength you need to make it through.

Peter learned this same principle when he walked with Jesus on the water. He was able to stay above the circumstances when he kept his focus on Jesus.

The Prize after the Trial

We enjoy sweeter fellowship with the Lord. I remember after my children received what my husband called "the board of education applied to the seat of learning," we would have a time of prayer and forgiveness. The countenance on their faces was so sweet and tender. It was a precious time as we enjoyed the peace that came as a result of the pain.

After a time of trial or correction, the Christian's countenance and spirit is more tender and sensitive to the Lord. The fellowship with God is sweeter than it was before!

> *But rejoice, inasmuch as ye are partakers of Christ's sufferings; that, when his glory shall be revealed, ye may be glad also with exceeding joy.*—1 PETER 4:13

We are useful to God. An instrument is useful only if it's in the right shape. A dull ax or a bent screwdriver needs attention, and so do we, if we are dull or bent in our spiritual lives. A good blacksmith keeps his tools in shape. So does God.

Should God place you through a trial, be thankful. It means He thinks you are still worth reshaping!

> *If a man therefore purge himself from these, he shall be a vessel unto honour, sanctified, and meet for the master's use, and prepared unto every good work.*—2 TIMOTHY 2:21

We learn patience. Even though we don't always like the process, the Bible tells us that trials produce patience.

> *Knowing this, that the trying of your faith worketh patience. But let patience have her perfect work, that ye may be perfect and entire, wanting nothing.*—JAMES 1:3–4

We experience peace. God promises His peace as a result of suffering. And God's peace is a peace that passes all understanding!

> *Be careful for nothing; but in every thing by prayer and supplication with thanksgiving let your requests be made known unto God. And the peace of God, which passeth all understanding, shall keep your hearts and minds through Christ Jesus.*—PHILIPPIANS 4:6-7

John 14:27 says, *"Peace I leave with you, my peace I give unto you...."* It's hard to imagine more difficult circumstances in which those words could be spoken. Jesus had taken a beating from the leaders of Israel—questioning, cross-examining, hostility, and anger. He could see in Peter's eyes the cloudy look of deception that would lead to defection and denial. He knew that Judas was betraying Him at that very moment. Talk about troubles! It was in the midst of this kind of terrible trouble that Jesus uttered these words about peace. How was He able to do that?

The answer lies in the fact that the peace of Jesus Christ was not based on His feelings, but on the clear conviction that God is sovereign and all-powerful. In addition, Jesus lived with confidence in God's timely intervention. How else could He offer peace on the night before His crucifixion knowing the trials He would go through as He became the substitutionary sacrifice for the sins of the whole world!

> God has not promised skies always blue,
> Flower-strewn pathways all our life through;
> God has not promised sun without rain,
> Joy without sorrow, peace without pain.
> But God has promised strength for the day,
> Rest for the labor, light for the way;
> Grace for the trials, help from above,
> Unfailing sympathy, undying love.
> —Source Unknown

A young woman went to her mother and told her how difficult things were in her life. She didn't know how she was going to make it, and she wanted to give up. She was tired of fighting and struggling. It seemed as one problem was solved, a new one arose.

Her mother took her to the kitchen where she filled three pots with water. She placed carrots in the first, eggs in the second, and ground coffee beans in the third. She let them boil without saying a word. In about twenty minutes, she turned off the burners. She fished out the carrots and placed them in a bowl. She pulled out the eggs and placed them in a second bowl. She poured the coffee into a third bowl. Turning to her daughter, she requested, "Tell me what you see." "Carrots, eggs, and coffee," the daughter replied.

The mother brought her closer and asked her to feel the carrots. The daughter did and noted that they were soft. Next, she had her daughter take an egg and break it. After pulling off the shell, she observed the hard-boiled egg. Finally, she had her daughter sip the coffee. The daughter smiled as she tasted its rich flavor.

The daughter then asked, "What's the point, Mother?" Her mother explained that each of these objects had faced the same adversity—boiling water—but each reacted differently. The carrot went in strong, hard, and unrelenting, but after being subjected to the boiling water, it softened and became weak. The egg had been fragile, its thin outer shell protecting its liquid interior. After sitting in the boiling water, its inside became hardened. The ground coffee beans were unique. After they were in the boiling water, they changed the water.

"Which are you the most like?" she asked her daughter. "When adversity knocks on your door, how do you respond? Are you a carrot, an egg, or a coffee bean?"

How do you respond to the challenges, trials and circumstances of your life? Are you like the carrot, seemingly strong until the pain of adversity comes, which makes you lose your strength and makes you soft and weak?

Are you like the egg that is soft and tender? But in the heat of a trial, has your heart become hardened?

The coffee bean changed the hot water, the very thing that brought the adversity. Also, the coffee bean released a fragrance that filled the room. Are you like the coffee bean? When things are at their worst, do you, by God's grace, improve the situation around you? Ask God to help you be that kind of Christian in times of difficulty.

Ask the Lord today to give you a new perspective on trials and testing, and determine to be a coffee bean Christian!

CONCLUSION

Little did I realize, when I accepted Christ as my Saviour, the wonderful life God would give me. Don't get me wrong. There have been many trials, challenges, and hurts along the way, but God's grace has turned every burden into a blessing and has shown me His purpose day by day.

God has a plan for you—a wonderful plan for your life. Jeremiah 29:11 says, *"For I know the thoughts that I think toward you, saith the LORD, thoughts of peace, and not of evil, to give you an expected end."* No one is insignificant to God.

It has been my prayer that this book would encourage you to find God's purpose for your life and run with it. I also hope this book has caused you to focus on Christ. It is a choice. Choose to make Him the focus of your life.

I pray that God will use the truths and lessons He has taught me to encourage you. I hope you will allow God to use you, bless you, and strengthen you each day as you live in obedience to Him.

Life is too short to spend it complaining. God's purpose for you is too special to miss. Allow God to be the center of your life, and begin living every day for His glory.

John 10:10 says, *"...I am come that they might have life, and that they might have it more abundantly."* Jesus came to give us abundant life. It is a promise we can claim. As you claim that promise and live surrendered to Him day by day, you too will discover that it really is a *wonderful* life!

NOTES

Chapter One

1.   W. A. Criswell, *Criswell's Guidebook for Pastors*, (Nashville, TN: Baptist Sunday School Board, 1980).

Chapter Two

2.   Elizabeth George, *A Woman's High Calling*, (Eugene, OR: Harvest House Publishers, 2001).

Chapter Four

3.   John W. Kennedy, *US News and World Report*, "Eye on the '90s," July 27, 1992.

Chapter Eleven

4.   Sylvia Gunter, *Prayer Portions*, (Murphy, OR: Castle Peak Editions, 1991).

Visit us online

strivingtogether.com

dailyintheword.org

wcbc.edu

lancasterbaptist.org

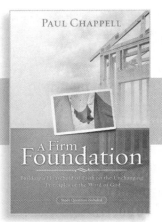

A Firm Foundation

In a culture that is redefining marriage and the family, you can build your family upon the firm foundation of God's Word! If you are determined to understand and follow God's design for your family, the pages of this book will establish your footing on solid ground! Includes study questions at the end of each chapter! (240 Pages, Paperback)

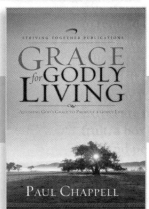

Grace for Godly Living

In these pages, you will discover that God's grace at work in your life will not only compel you to live a godly lifestyle, but it will give you a spiritual maturity and humility toward those who do not. (160 Pages, Hardback)

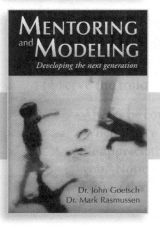

Mentoring and Modeling

Mentoring and Modeling is a primer that can help those who are working with young people to do so in an effective way. Former President Ronald Reagan said, "We don't expect children to discover the principles of calculus on their own, but some would give them no guidance when it comes to ethics, morality, and values." (192 Pages, Paperback)

done.

Specifically created to be placed into the hands of an unsaved person and a perfect gift for first-time church visitors, this new mini book explains the Gospel in crystal clear terms. The reader will journey step by step through biblical reasoning that concludes at the Cross and a moment of decision. This tool will empower your whole church family to share the Gospel with anyone! (100 pages, Mini Paperback)

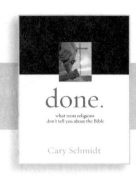

Your Pastor and You

Wise Christians find and establish strong relationships with godly pastors and choose to fight for those relationships. They encourage their pastors, accept his spiritual watchcare in their lives, and support him in his call to serve God. (48 pages, Mini Paperback)

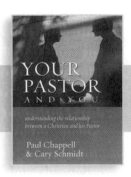

A Maze of Grace

If you are, or someone you love is, enduring a season of suffering, this little booklet will provide a cup of fresh water for the journey. Each chapter shares God's wisdom, encouragement, and insight. Each turn of the page will bring fresh hope and trust in the unseen hand of a loving God. (64 pages, Mini Paperback)